SOME COMMON
BASIC
PROGRAMS
3RD EDITION

SOME COMMON
BASIC
PROGRAMS
3RD EDITION

Lon Poole
Mary Borchers

OSBORNE/McGraw-Hill
Berkeley, California

Published by
OSBORNE/McGraw-Hill
630 Bancroft Way
Berkeley, California 94710
U.S.A.

For information on translations and book distributors outside of the U.S.A.,
please write OSBORNE/McGraw-Hill.

SOME COMMON BASIC PROGRAMS, 3RD EDITION

3 4 5 6 7 8 9 0 GBGB   8 7 6 5 4 3 2 1 0

ISBN 0-931988-06-3

DISCLAIMER OF WARRANTIES AND LIMITATION OF LIABILITIES

Table of Contents

Table of Contents (Continued)

Introduction

This book describes a number of programs, written in the BASIC[1] programming language. These programs perform a variety of common, practical tasks. The programs are written in a restricted subset of standard BASIC that is compatible with many versions of BASIC now available to microcomputer users.

You can use this book whether or not you know how to write programs in BASIC.

We do not teach you how to program in BASIC; there are probably hundreds of books trying to do that. But we do describe progams carefully and include user examples with the program listings. So if you are not familiar with BASIC, simply copy the program listings into your computer; then run the programs as illustrated in the examples.

Remarks are included in the listings to help BASIC programmers understand how each program works. They will also assist you in identifying parts of programs that you may be able to use in other programs you write. Remark statements precede the line(s) on which they comment. *REM statements should be omitted when you enter programs, since they are ignored by the computer and simply use up memory.*

Options are also included with some programs. An option is an alteration which changes the input or output format of the original program. Options may suggest ways in which you can further alter the programs. We have included a brief description, example, sample run and partial listing of each option. The partial listing includes those program statements which are changed when going from the original program to the optional program. Lines which must be altered, added or deleted are shaded in both listings.

All programs can be run using a Teletype[2] or similar input/output device with a line width as short as 72 characters. If the line width on your output device is less than 72 characters, you may want to alter the print statements within programs that print longer lines.

Certain programs will require additional programming if you use a CRT display or separate printing device for output. If using a CRT, you will probably want to put a pause in some programs after displaying one screenful of data; otherwise, the data will be displayed faster than you can read it. If using a separate printing device for your output, you may need to add print device select statements to the programs.

All programs in this book have been tested, run and listed on a Wang 2200 computer system. They have also been tested and run on a Commodore PET[3]. Some of this testing was with programs modified for better efficiency on the PET.

BASIC Compatibility

Readers of the first and second editions of this book have helped locate typographical and programming errors and have informed us of some compatibility problems for users with different BASICs. For this third edition we have done some reprogramming to eliminate errors and help solve the compatibility problems. Even so, you should be aware of some general compatibility problems which may occur.

1) Some programs may branch out of a FOR/NEXT loop before its iteration is complete. If branching out in the middle of a FOR/NEXT loop causes an error in your BASIC, you can change the FOR/NEXT loop at that point to branch to the NEXT statement, avoiding any program statements which would alter other variable values as the loop completes itself.

2) When a FOR/NEXT loop is completed, the index variable should remain set to its highest value when the progam resumes after the loop. For example, in the following program the value of I at line 30 should be 10.

```
10 FOR I = 1 TO 10
20 NEXT I
30 PRINT I
```

---

[1]BASIC is a registered trademark of the Trustees of Dartmouth College.
[2]Teletype is a registered trademark of the Teletype Corporation.
[3]PET is a registered trademark of Commodore, Inc.

Your BASIC may say I = 11 at line 30. To fix this, add a new line after the NEXT statement to decrement the index variable by one. In the above program, add the following:

$$25 \ I = I - 1$$

If you have a BASIC which does *not* have a FOR/NEXT index variable keep its value outside the loop, you will have to set the variable equal to the end value of the loop once outside the loop (you need to do this only if that index variable value is used later in the program).

3) One variation of the RESTORE command is RESTORE *n*, where *n* refers to the *n*th item on the data list, and this *n*th item is to be read in the next READ statement. If your BASIC does not accept RESTORE *n*, change that part of the program to RESTORE, then loop to read data to the *n*th item.

4) If your BASIC does not set all variables to zero for each RUN (unless another value is specified in a statement), then you will have to write statements to initialize each variable to zero at the beginning of each program.

5) Some programs use DEF FNR (). If not implemented, substitute this expression (with appropriate variable) for each callout of FNR.

6) Some programs use the TAB function with the PRINT statement. You can usually replace it with a string of blanks of the appropriate length. For instance, PRINT TAB (5); A1 could be PRINT "   "; A1.

Program Errors

If you encounter an error or program difficulty which you believe is not your fault, we would like to hear about it. Please write the authors in care of the publishers, and include the followng information:

1) description of the error

2) data entered which caused the error

3) source listing of your program, from your computer (if possible)

4) any corrections you have

We appreciate your help in creating a book of tested BASIC programs that *anyone* can use.

Future Value of an Investment

This program calculates a future value of an investment when interest is a factor. You must provide the amount of the initial investment, the nominal interest rate, the number of compounding periods per year and the number of years of investment.

Assuming there are no additional deposits and no withdrawals, the future value is based on the following formula:

$$T = P(1 + i/N)^{N \cdot Y}$$

where: T = total value after Y years (future value)
P = initial investment
i = nominal interest rate
N = number of compounding period per year
Y = number of years

Examples:

Carl makes an investment of $6800.00 at 9.5%. If interest is compounded quarterly, what will be the value of Carl's investment in 10 years?

Mr. Smith purchases a piece of property for $16,050.00. The value of property is rising at an average of 7% per year. What may Mr. Smith expect his property to be worth in 5½ years?

```
:RUN
FUTURE VALUE OF AN INVESTMENT

INITIAL INVESTMENT? 6800
NOMINAL INTEREST RATE? 9.5
NUMBER OF COMPOUNDING PERIODS PER YEAR? 4
NUMBER OF YEARS? 10
FUTURE VALUE=$ 17388.64

MORE DATA? (1=YES,0=NO)? 1

INITIAL INVESTMENT? 16050
NOMINAL INTEREST RATE? 7
NUMBER OF COMPOUNDING PERIODS PER YEAR? 1
NUMBER OF YEARS? 5.5
FUTURE VALUE=$ 23285.51

MORE DATA? (1=YES,0=NO)? 0

END PROGRAM


PROGRAM LISTING

   10   PRINT "FUTURE VALUE OF AN INVESTMENT"
   20   PRINT
   29   REM - STATEMENTS 30 TO 100 REQUEST USER INPUT
   30   PRINT "INITIAL INVESTMENT";
   40   INPUT P
   50   PRINT "NOMINAL INTEREST RATE";
```

```
60    INPUT I
70    PRINT "NUMBER OF COMPOUNDING PERIODS PER YEAR";
80    INPUT N
90    PRINT "NUMBER OF YEARS";
100   INPUT Y
108   REM - CALCULATE INTEREST RATE PER PERIOD;
109   REM - CONVERT FROM PERCENT TO DECIMAL
110   I=I/N/100
119   REM - CALCULATE FUTURE VALUE BY FORMULA
120   T=P*(1+I)^(N*Y)
129   REM - ROUND OFF TO NEAREST CENT, PRINT
130   PRINT "FUTURE VALUE=$"; INT(T*100+.5)/100
139   REM - PRINT BLANK LINE TO SEPARATE DATA FROM QUESTION
140   PRINT
149   REM - RESTART OR END PROGRAM? USER INPUT REQUIRED
150   PRINT "MORE DATA? (1=YES,0=NO)";
160   INPUT X
170   IF X=1  THEN   20
180   END
```

OPTION

This program allows you to enter a term of investment in whole years or decimal parts only. In some cases you may wish to enter the term of investment in years and months rather than just years. The program changes necessary follow the example listed below.

Example:

Herb invests $12,000.00 at 8% interest. Interest is compounded quarterly. What is the value of his investment at the end of 10 years and 7 months?

```
:RUN
FUTURE VALUE OF AN INVESTMENT

INITIAL INVESTMENT? 12000
NOMINAL INTEREST RATE? 8
NUMBER OF COMPOUNDING PERIODS PER YEAR? 4
NUMBER OF YEARS, MONTHS? 10,7
FUTURE VALUE=$ 27749.5

MORE DATA? (1=YES,0=NO)? 0

END PROGRAM


PROGRAM LISTING

    1    REM - OPTION 90-105
   10    PRINT "FUTURE VALUE OF AN INVESTMENT"
   :
   80    INPUT N
   90    PRINT "NUMBER OF YEARS, MONTHS";
  100    INPUT Y0,M
  104    REM - CALCULATE YEARS FROM YEARS AND MONTHS
  105    Y=(12*Y0+M)/12
  108    REM - CALCULATE INTEREST RATE PER PERIOD;
   :
  180    END
```

Future Value of Regular Deposits (Annuity)

This program calculates a future value when deposits are made regularly. All deposits are equal. You must provide the amount of each deposit, the number of deposits per year, the number of years, and the nominal interest rate.

Assuming that interest is compounded with each deposit, the calculation is based on the following formula:

$$T = R \cdot \left(\frac{(1 + i/N)^{N \cdot Y} - 1}{i/N} \right)$$

where:
T = total value after Y years (future value)
R = amount of regular deposits
N = number of deposits per year
Y = number of years
i = nominal interest rate

Examples:

$50.00 is transferred each month from Matt's checking account to a Christmas Club savings account with 5% interest. How much will Matt receive at the end of the year?

Tim makes annuity payments of $175.00. The interest is 5.5%. What amount will Tim have accumulated in 15 years?

```
:RUN
FUTURE VALUE OF REGULAR DEPOSITS (ANNUITY)

AMOUNT OF REGULAR DEPOSITS? 50
NOMINAL INTEREST RATE? 5
NUMBER OF DEPOSITS PER YEAR? 12
NUMBER OF YEARS? 1
FUTURE VALUE = $ 613.94

MORE DATA? (1=YES, 0=NO)? 1

AMOUNT OF REGULAR DEPOSITS? 175
NOMINAL INTEREST RATE? 5.5
NUMBER OF DEPOSITS PER YEAR? 1
NUMBER OF YEARS? 15
FUTURE VALUE = $ 3921.52

MORE DATA? (1=YES, 0=NO)? 0

END PROGRAM
```

```
PROGRAM LISTING

10   PRINT "FUTURE VALUE OF REGULAR DEPOSITS (ANNUITY)"
20   PRINT
29   REM - STATEMENTS 30 TO 100 REQUEST USER INPUT
30   PRINT "AMOUNT OF REGULAR DEPOSITS";
40   INPUT R
50   PRINT "NOMINAL INTEREST RATE";
```

```
 60    INPUT I
 70    PRINT "NUMBER OF DEPOSITS PER YEAR";
 80    INPUT N
 90    PRINT "NUMBER OF YEARS";
100    INPUT Y
108    REM - CALCULATE INTEREST RATE PER DEPOSIT,
109    REM - CONVERT FROM PERCENT TO DECIMAL
110    I=I/N/100
119    REM - CALCULATE FUTURE VALUE BY FORMULA
120    T=R*((1+I)^(N*Y)-1)/I
129    REM - ROUND OFF TO NEAREST CENT, PRINT
130    PRINT "FUTURE VALUE = $"; INT(T*100+.5)/100
139    REM - PRINT BLANK LINE TO SEPARATE DATA FROM QUESTION
140    PRINT
149    REM - RESTART OR END PROGRAM?  USER INPUT REQUIRED
150    PRINT "MORE DATA? (1=YES, 0=NO)";
160    INPUT X
170    IF X=1  THEN   20
180    END
```

OPTION

You may wish to enter the term of investment in years and months rather than years. The program changes necessary are listed following the example below.

Example:

How much will Ron receive in 10 years and 5 months if he transfers $50.00 each month into a trust fund with 5% interest?

```
:RUN
FUTURE VALUE OF REGULAR DEPOSITS (ANNUITY)

AMOUNT OF REGULAR DEPOSITS? 50
NOMINAL INTEREST RATE? 5
NUMBER OF DEPOSITS PER YEAR? 12
NUMBER OF YEARS, MONTHS? 10,5
FUTURE VALUE = $ 8179.31

MORE DATA? (1=YES, 0=NO)? 0

END PROGRAM


PROGRAM LISTING

   1   REM - OPTION 90-105
  10   PRINT "FUTURE VALUE OF REGULAR DEPOSITS (ANNUITY)"
       :
  80   INPUT N
  90   PRINT "NUMBER OF YEARS, MONTHS";
 100   INPUT Y0,M
 104   REM - CALCULATE YEARS FROM YEARS AND MONTHS
 105   Y=(12*Y0+M)/12
 108   REM - CALCULATE INTEREST RATE PER DEPOSIT,
       :
 180   END
```

4

Regular Deposits

This program calculates the amount required as a regular deposit to provide a stated future value in a specified time period. All deposits are equal. It is necessary for you to supply the future value, the nominal interest rate, the number of deposits per year and the number of years.

The calculation for regular deposits is based on the following formula:

$$R = T \left(\frac{i/N}{(1+i/N)^{N \cdot Y} - 1} \right)$$

where:
- R = amount of regular deposit
- T = future value
- i = nominal interest rate
- N = number of deposits per year
- Y = number of years

Example:

Mary would like $1000.00 at the end of one year in a savings account. How much must she deposit each month at 8% interest to achieve this?

```
:RUN
REGULAR DEPOSITS

TOTAL VALUE AFTER Y YEARS? 1000
NOMINAL INTEREST RATE? 8
NUMBER OF DEPOSITS PER YEAR? 12
NUMBER OF YEARS? 1
REGULAR DEPOSITS = $ 80.32

MORE DATA?(1=YES,0=NO)? 0

END PROGRAM


PROGRAM LISTING

   10   PRINT "REGULAR DEPOSITS"
   20   PRINT
   29   REM - STATEMENTS 30 TO 100 REQUEST USER INPUT
   30   PRINT "TOTAL VALUE AFTER Y YEARS";
   40   INPUT T
   50   PRINT "NOMINAL INTEREST RATE";
   60   INPUT I
   70   PRINT "NUMBER OF DEPOSITS PER YEAR";
   80   INPUT N
   90   PRINT "NUMBER OF YEARS";
  100   INPUT Y
  108   REM - CALCULATE INTEREST RATE PER DEPOSIT;
  109   REM - CONVERT FROM PERCENT TO DECIMAL
  110   I=I/N/100
```

```
119   REM - CALCULATE AMOUNT OF REGULAR DEPOSIT BY FORMULA.
120   R=T*I/((I+1)↑(N*Y)-1)
129   REM - ROUND OFF TO NEAREST CENT, PRINT
130   PRINT "REGULAR DEPOSITS = $";INT(R*100+.5)/100
139   REM - PRINT BLANK LINE TO SEPARATE DATA FROM QUESTION
140   PRINT
149   REM - RESTART OR END PROGRAM? USER INPUT REQUIRED
150   PRINT "MORE DATA?(1=YES,0=NO)";
160   INPUT X
170   IF X=1   THEN    20
180   END
```

OPTION

You may wish to enter the term of investment in years and months rather than years. The program changes necessary are listed following the example below.

Example:

Ed would like to save $2000.00 for a new motorcycle. He would like to achieve this amount in 1 year and 5 months. How much must he deposit each month if his interest is 8%?

```
:RUN
REGULAR DEPOSITS

TOTAL VALUE AFTER Y YEARS? 2000
NOMINAL INTEREST RATE? 8
NUMBER OF DEPOSITS PER YEAR? 12
NUMBER OF YEARS, MONTHS? 1,5
REGULAR DEPOSITS = $ 111.5

MORE DATA?(1=YES,0=NO)? 0

END PROGRAM
```

```
PROGRAM LISTING

    1   REM - OPTION 90-105
   10   PRINT "REGULAR DEPOSITS"
    ⋮
   80   INPUT N
   90   PRINT "NUMBER OF YEARS, MONTHS";
  100   INPUT Y0,M
  104   REM - CALCULATE YEARS FROM YEARS AND MONTHS
  105   Y=(12*Y0+M)/12
  108   REM - CALCULATE INTEREST RATE PER DEPOSIT;
    ⋮
  180   END
```

Regular Withdrawals from an Investment

This program calculates the maximum amount which may be withdrawn regularly from an investment over a specified time period. All withdrawals are assumed to be equal. You must provide the amount of the initial investment, the nominal interest rate, the number of withdrawals per year and the number of years.

The maximum amount of withdrawals is calculated by the following formula:

$$R = P \left(\frac{i/N}{(1 + i/N)^{N \cdot Y} - 1} \; + \; \frac{i}{N} \right)$$

where: R = amount of regular withdrawal
P = initial investment
i = nominal interest rate
N = number of withdrawals per year
Y = number of years

Because this program calculates a maximum amount, a balance of $0.00 will be left in your account at the end of the time period. You may withdraw any lesser amount under the same specifications and leave a remaining balance in your account.

Example:

David invests $8000.00 at 9.5%. He plans to make regular withdrawals every month for ten years, leaving nothing at the end. How much should he withdraw each time?

```
:RUN
REGULAR WITHDRAWALS FROM AN INVESTMENT

INITIAL INVESTMENT? 8000
NOMINAL INTEREST RATE? 9.5
NUMBER OF WITHDRAWALS PER YEAR? 12
NUMBER OF YEARS? 10
AMOUNT OF EACH WITHDRAWAL = $ 103.52

MORE DATA?(1=YES,0=NO)? 0

END PROGRAM
```

PROGRAM LISTING

```
10    PRINT "REGULAR WITHDRAWALS FROM AN INVESTMENT"
20    PRINT
29    REM - STATEMENTS 30 TO 100 REQUEST USER INPUT
30    PRINT "INITIAL INVESTMENT";
40    INPUT P
50    PRINT "NOMINAL INTEREST RATE";
60    INPUT I
70    PRINT "NUMBER OF WITHDRAWALS PER YEAR";
80    INPUT N
90    PRINT "NUMBER OF YEARS";
100   INPUT Y
```

```
108   REM - CALCULATE INTEREST RATE PER. WITHDRAWAL;
109   REM - CONVERT FROM PERCENT TO DECIMAL
110   I=I/N/100
119   REM - CALCULATE REGULAR WITHDRAWAL BY FORMULA
120   R=P*(I/((1+I)^(N*Y)-1)+I)
129   REM - ROUND OFF TO NEAREST CENT, PRINT
130   PRINT "AMOUNT OF EACH WITHDRAWAL = $"; INT(R*100+.5)/100
139   REM - PRINT BLANK LINE TO SEPARATE QUESTION FROM DATA
140   PRINT
149   REM - RESTART OR END PROGRAM?
150   PRINT "MORE DATA?(1=YES,0=NO)";
160   INPUT X
170   IF X=1  THEN   20
180   END
```

OPTION

It may be more convenient to enter the period of investment in years and months rather than just years. The program changes necessary are listed following the example below.

Example:

How much could be withdrawn each week if you have an investment of $8000.00 at 9.5% interest to be withdrawn from for 10 years and 5 months?

```
:RUN
REGULAR WITHDRAWALS FROM AN INVESTMENT

INITIAL INVESTMENT? 8000
NOMINAL INTEREST RATE? 9.5
NUMBER OF WITHDRAWALS PER YEAR? 52
NUMBER OF YEARS, MONTHS? 10,5
AMOUNT OF EACH WITHDRAWAL = $ 23.28

MORE DATA?(1=YES,0=NO)? 0

END PROGRAM
```

```
PROGRAM LISTING

    1   REM - OPTION 90-105
   10   PRINT "REGULAR WITHDRAWALS FROM AN INVESTMENT"
    .
    .
   80   INPUT N
   90   PRINT "NUMBER OF YEARS, MONTHS";
  100   INPUT Y0,M
  104   REM - CALCULATE YEARS FROM YEARS AND MONTHS
  105   Y=(12*Y0+M)/12
  108   REM - CALCULATE INTEREST RATE PER WITHDRAWAL;
    .
    .
  180   END
```

Initial Investment

This program calculates the investment necessary to provide a stated future value in a specified time period. You must enter the future value of the investment, the number of years of investment, the number of compounding periods per year and the nominal interest rate.

The formula used to calculate the initial investment is as follows:

$$P = \frac{T}{(1 + i/N)^{N \cdot Y}}$$

where:
P = initial investment
T = future value
N = number of compounding periods per year
Y = number of years
i = nominal interest rate

Examples:

How much must you invest at 8.5% to produce $10,000.00 at the end of 10 years if interest is compounded quarterly?

Merchant Savings wishes to sell a bond which will be worth $5000.00 five years from the purchase date. Interest will be 7.9% compounded daily. How much must the bank charge for the bond?

```
:RUN
INITIAL INVESTMENT

TOTAL VALUE AFTER Y YEARS? 10000
NUMBER OF COMPOUNDING PERIODS PER YEAR? 4
NUMBER OF YEARS? 10
NOMINAL INTEREST RATE? 8.5
INITIAL INVESTMENT = $ 4312.33

MORE DATA? (1=YES,0=NO)? 1

TOTAL VALUE AFTER Y YEARS? 5000
NUMBER OF COMPOUNDING PERIODS PER YEAR? 365
NUMBER OF YEARS? 5
NOMINAL INTEREST RATE? 7.9
INITIAL INVESTMENT = $ 3368.54

MORE DATA? (1=YES,0=NO)? 0

END PROGRAM
```

```
PROGRAM LISTING

10   PRINT "INITIAL INVESTMENT"
20   PRINT
29   REM - STATEMENTS 30 TO 100 REQUEST USER INPUT
30   PRINT "TOTAL VALUE AFTER Y YEARS";
40   INPUT T
```

```
50    PRINT "NUMBER OF COMPOUNDING PERIODS PER YEAR";
60    INPUT N
70    PRINT "NUMBER OF YEARS";
80    INPUT Y
90    PRINT "NOMINAL INTEREST RATE";
100   INPUT I
108   REM - CALCULATE INTEREST RATE PER PERIOD;
109   REM - CONVERT FROM % TO DECIMAL
110   I=I/N/100
119   REM - CALCULATE INITIAL INVESTMENT BY FORMULA
120   P=T/(1+I)↑(N*Y)
129   REM - ROUND OFF TO NEAREST CENT, PRINT
130   PRINT "INITIAL INVESTMENT = $";INT(P*100+.5)/100
139   REM - PRINT BLANK LINE TO SEPARATE DATA FROM QUESTION
140   PRINT
149   REM - RESTART OR END PROGRAM? USER INPUT REQUIRED
150   PRINT "MORE DATA? (1=YES,0=NO)";
160   INPUT X
170   IF X=1  THEN   20
180   END
```

OPTION

The program above allows you to enter a period of investment of whole years and decimal parts only. You may wish to enter the period of investment in years and months rather than just years. The program changes necessary are listed following the example below.

Example:

Mary wishes to invest a sum in a savings bank. In 3 years and 8 months she would like to have $4000.00 in her account. If 8% interest is compounded monthly, what amount must Mary invest?

```
:RUN
INITIAL INVESTMENT

TOTAL VALUE AFTER Y YEARS? 4000
NUMBER OF COMPOUNDING PERIODS PER YEAR? 12
NUMBER OF YEARS, MONTHS? 3,8
NOMINAL INTEREST RATE? 8
INITIAL INVESTMENT = $ 2986

MORE DATA? (1=YES,0=NO)? 0

END PROGRAM


PROGRAM LISTING

  1   REM - OPTION 70-85
 10   PRINT "INITIAL INVESTMENT"
      .
      .
      .
 60   INPUT N
 70   PRINT "NUMBER OF YEARS, MONTHS";
 80   INPUT Y0,M
 84   REM - CALCULATE YEARS FROM YEARS AND MONTHS
 85   Y=(12*Y0+M)/12
 90   PRINT "NOMINAL INTEREST RATE";
      .
      .
      .
180   END
```

Minimum Investment for Withdrawals

This program calculates the minimum investment required to allow regular withdrawals over a specified time period. The amount calculated is dependent upon the amount of each withdrawal, the number of withdrawals per year, the number of years, and the nominal interest rate on the investment. All withdrawals are equal.

Only the least amount necessary for your investment is calculated; the program assumes a balance of $0.00 to be left at the end of the time period. Any investment larger than the amount calculated will also enable you to withdraw the desired amount, but leave a remaining balance.

Assuming that interest is compounded with each withdrawal, the calculation is based on the following formula:

$$P = \frac{R \cdot N}{i} \left(1 - \frac{1}{(1 + i/N)^{N \cdot Y}} \right)$$

where: P = initial investment
R = amount of regular withdrawal
i = nominal interest rate
N = number of withdrawals per year
Y = number of years

Example:

How much must you invest at 6% interest to allow monthly withdrawals of $100.00 for 5 years?

```
:RUN
MINIMUM INVESTMENT FOR WITHDRAWALS

AMOUNT OF WITHDRAWALS? 100
NOMINAL INTEREST RATE? 6
NUMBER OF WITHDRAWALS PER YEAR? 12
NUMBER OF YEARS? 5
MINIMUM INVESTMENT = $ 5172.55

MORE DATA (1=YES, 0=NO)? 0

END PROGRAM
```

PROGRAM LISTING

```
10    PRINT "MINIMUM INVESTMENT FOR WITHDRAWALS"
20    PRINT
29    REM - STATEMENTS 30 TO 100 REQUEST USER INPUT
30    PRINT "AMOUNT OF WITHDRAWALS";
40    INPUT R
50    PRINT "NOMINAL INTEREST RATE";
60    INPUT I
70    PRINT "NUMBER OF WITHDRAWALS PER YEAR";
80    INPUT N
90    PRINT "NUMBER OF YEARS";
100   INPUT Y
```

```
109   REM - CONVERT FROM PERCENT TO DECIMAL
110   I=I/100
119   REM - CALCULATE MINIMUM INVESTMENT BY FORMULA
120   P=R*N/I*(1-1/((1+I/N)↑(N*Y)))
129   REM - ROUND OFF TO NEAREST CENT, PRINT
130   PRINT "MINIMUM INVESTMENT = $";INT(100*P+.5)/100
139   REM - PRINT BLANK LINE TO SEPARATE DATA FROM QUESTION
140   PRINT
149   REM - RESTART OR END PROGRAM? USER INPUT REQUIRED
150   PRINT "MORE DATA (1=YES, 0=NO)";
160   INPUT X
170   IF X=1  THEN   20
180   END
```

OPTION

It may be more convenient to enter the term of investment in years and months rather than years. The program changes necessary are listed following the example below.

Example:

Tony withdrew $250.00 monthly for 6 years and 5 months. How much was his initial investment at 6% interest?

```
:RUN
MINIMUM INVESTMENT FOR WITHDRAWALS

AMOUNT OF WITHDRAWALS? 250
NOMINAL INTEREST RATE? 6
NUMBER OF WITHDRAWALS PER YEAR? 12
NUMBER OF YEARS, MONTHS? 6,5
MINIMUM INVESTMENT = $ 15944.81

MORE DATA (1=YES, 0=NO)? 0

END PROGRAM


PROGRAM LISTING

  1   REM - OPTION 90-105
 10   PRINT "MINIMUM INVESTMENT FOR WITHDRAWALS"
  ⋮
 80   INPUT N
 90   PRINT "NUMBER OF YEARS, MONTHS";
100   INPUT Y0,M
104   REM - CALCULATE YEARS FROM YEARS AND MONTHS
105   Y=(12*Y0+M)/12
109   REM - CONVERT FROM PERCENT TO DECIMAL
  ⋮
180   END
```

Nominal Interest Rate on Investments

This program calculates the nominal interest rate for a known initial investment which amounts to a known future value in a specified period of time. The nominal interest rate is usually subdivided for compounding purposes.

"Nominal Interest Rate" is based on the following formula:

$$i = N(T/P)^{\frac{1}{N \cdot Y}} - N$$

where:
- i = nominal interest rate
- P = initial investment
- T = future value
- N = number of compounding periods per year
- Y = number of years

The nominal interest rate is expressed as a yearly rate even though the interest rate used when compounding interest is $\frac{i}{N}$. The nominal interest rate will be less than the effective interest rate when interest is compounded more than once a year. This is because the nominal rate stated does not take into account interest compounded on interest earned in earlier periods of each year. For example, the schedule of earned interest on $100.00 at 5% compounded quarterly would be:

PERIOD	BALANCE		$\dfrac{i/100}{N}$		INTEREST	NEW BALANCE
1	$100.00	·	.0125	=	$1.25	$101.25
2	$101.25	·	.0125	=	$1.27	$102.52
3	$102.52	·	.0125	=	$1.28	$103.80
4	$103.80	·	.0125	=	$1.30	$105.10

The *effective* interest rate in the example is 5.1%, although the *nominal* rate is 5%.

Examples:

Jane invests $945.00 in a savings bank. Four and a half years later her investment amounts to $1309.79. If interest is compounded monthly, what is the nominal interest rate offered by the bank?

Dick invests $3,000.00. Ten years later he has earned $1,576.00 in interest. If interest is compounded each month, what is the nominal interest rate on the account?

```
:RUN
NOMINAL INTEREST RATE ON INVESTMENTS

PRINCIPAL? 945
TOTAL VALUE? 1309.79
NUMBER OF YEARS? 4.5
NUMBER OF COMPOUNDING PERIODS PER YEAR? 12
NOMINAL INTEREST RATE= 7.2761298 %

MORE DATA: (1=YES,0=NO)? 1

PRINCIPAL? 3000
TOTAL VALUE? 4576
NUMBER OF YEARS? 10
```

NUMBER OF COMPOUNDING PERIODS PER YEAR? 12
NOMINAL INTEREST RATE= 4.22956608 %

MORE DATA: (1=YES,0=NO)? 0

END PROGRAM

PROGRAM LISTING

```
 10    PRINT "NOMINAL INTEREST RATE ON INVESTMENTS"
 20    PRINT
 29    REM - STATEMENTS 30 TO 100 REQUEST USER INPUT
 30    PRINT "PRINCIPAL";
 40    INPUT P
 50    PRINT "TOTAL VALUE";
 60    INPUT T
 70    PRINT "NUMBER OF YEARS";
 80    INPUT Y
 90    PRINT "NUMBER OF COMPOUNDING PERIODS PER YEAR";
100    INPUT N
109    REM - CALCULATE NOMINAL INTEREST RATE BY FORMULA, PRINT
110    I2=N*((T/P)↑(1/(N*Y))-1)*100
120    PRINT "NOMINAL INTEREST RATE=";I2;"%"
129    REM - PRINT BLANK LINE TO SEPARATE DATA FROM QUESTION
130    PRINT
139    REM - RESTART OR END PROGRAM? USER INPUT REQUIRED
140    PRINT "MORE DATA: (1=YES,0=NO)";
150    INPUT X
160    IF X=1  THEN    20
170    END
```

Effective Interest Rate on Investments

This program calculates the effective interest rate for a known initial investment which amounts to a known future value in a specified period of time. This rate expresses the actual rate of interest earned annually on the investment.

The effective interest rate is calculated by the following formula:

$$\text{effective interest rate} = \left(\frac{\text{future value}}{\text{initial investment}} \right)^{1/\text{years}} - 1$$

You may calculate the effective interest rate on amounts you have already invested and accrued interest. Or you may calculate the effective interest rate necessary to enable a principal to reach a hypothetical value in a specified amount of time. For instance, if you invest $5000.00 in a bank and desire $6800.00 after six years, you will predict the effective interest rate the bank must pay in order to achieve this.

"Effective Interest Rate" may also be used to calculate the effective percent of depreciation of an investment. Take your car, for example. If you bought it for $7534.00 and sold it for $3555.00 three years later, you will find that its actual depreciation (a negative interest rate) was approximately 22% each year.

Examples:

Jane deposits $945.00 in a savings bank. Four and a half years later her account has $1309.79. What actual percent of her initial investment did the bank pay annually?

Dick bought his car in 1970 for $7534.84 and sold it in 1973 for $3555.00. What was its effective rate of depreciation?

```
:RUN
EFFECTIVE INTEREST RATE ON INVESTMENTS

INITIAL INVESTMENT? 945
TOTAL VALUE AFTER Y YEARS? 1309.79
NUMBER OF YEARS? 4.5
ANNUAL INTEREST RATE = 7.5237528 %

MORE DATA? (1=YES,0=NO)? 1

INITIAL INVESTMENT? 7534.84
TOTAL VALUE AFTER Y YEARS? 3555
NUMBER OF YEARS? 3
ANNUAL INTEREST RATE =-22.150614266 %

MORE DATA? (1=YES,0=NO)? 0

END PROGRAM
```

```
 10    PRINT "EFFECTIVE INTEREST RATE ON INVESTMENTS"
 20    PRINT
 29    REM - STATEMENTS 30-80 REQUEST USER INPUT
 30    PRINT "INITIAL INVESTMENT";
 40    INPUT P
 50    PRINT "TOTAL VALUE AFTER Y YEARS";
 60    INPUT T
 70    PRINT "NUMBER OF YEARS";
 80    INPUT Y
 89    REM - CALCULATE EFFECTIVE INTEREST RATE, PRINT
 90    PRINT "ANNUAL INTEREST RATE =";((T/P)↑(1/Y)-1)*100;"%"
 99    REM - PRINT BLANK LINE TO SEPARATE DATA FROM QUESTION
100    PRINT
109    REM - RESTART OR END PROGRAM?
110    PRINT "MORE DATA? (1=YES,0=NO)";
120    INPUT X
130    IF X=1  THEN   20
140    END
```

Earned Interest Table

This program calculates and prints an earned interest table for investments. The schedule contains the following outputs:

1) Periodic balance
2) Interest accumulated between two periods
3) Total interest accumulated
4) Effective interest rate

These outputs may be calculated for a single investment or for an initial investment with regular deposits or withdrawals. If the table is to be tabulated for a single investment, you must provide the amount of the initial investment, the nominal interest rate, and the number of compounding periods per year. Your new balance will be printed a maximum of four times per year. If interest is compounded less than four times per year, your new balance will be posted with each interest computation.

If the table is tabulated for regular deposits or withdrawals, you must provide the amount of the initial investment, the nominal interest rate, the number of deposits or withdrawals per year and their amount. In this case it is assumed interest is compounded daily (360-day year). Your new balance will be printed at each deposit or withdrawal.

Examples:

Sally invests $2000.00 at 9.5% in a trust fund for ten years. Interest is compounded monthly. What is her yearly balance and earned interest for the last two years?

John deposits $1000.00 at 8% in a passbook savings account. From each monthly paycheck $50.00 is deposited in this account. What is the earned interest table for the first year of this account?

Ted deposits $1000.00 at 8% in his savings. Each quarter he withdraws $150.00. What is the earned interest table for year one of this account?

```
:RUN
EARNED INTEREST TABLE

PRINCIPAL? 2000
NOMINAL INTEREST RATE? 9.5
NUMBER OF DEPOSITS/WITHDRAWALS PER YEAR? 0
NUMBER OF COMPOUNDING PERIODS PER YEAR? 12
START WITH WHAT YEAR? 9
END PRINTING WITH WHAT YEAR? 10
```

```
                    EARNED INTEREST TABLE
     PRINCIPAL $ 2000        AT 9.5 % NOMINAL        FOR 10 YEARS
                EFFECTIVE INTEREST RATE 9.92 % PER YEAR


   YEAR           BALANCE           INTEREST          ACCUM.INTEREST

   9               4365.87           2365.86           2365.87
                   4470.38           104.51            2470.38
                   4577.39           107.01            2577.39
                   4686.97           109.58            2686.97


   10              4799.17           112.2             2799.17
                   4914.06           114.89            2914.06
                   5031.7            117.64            3031.7
                   5152.15           120.45            3152.15


CHANGE DATA AND RECOMPUTE? (1=YES, 0=NO)? 1



PRINCIPAL? 1000
NOMINAL INTEREST RATE? 8
NUMBER OF DEPOSITS/WITHDRAWALS PER YEAR? 12
AMOUNT OF DEPOSIT/WITHDRAWAL? 50
START WITH WHAT YEAR? 1
END PRINTING WITH WHAT YEAR? 1


                    EARNED INTEREST TABLE
     PRINCIPAL $ 1000        AT 8 % NOMINAL        FOR 1 YEARS
     REGULAR DEPOSIT/WITHDRAWAL $ 50        12   TIMES PER YEAR
                EFFECTIVE INTEREST RATE 8.33 % PER YEAR


   YEAR           BALANCE           INTEREST          ACCUM.INTEREST

   1               1056.7            6.7               6.7
                   1113.78           7.08              13.78
                   1171.24           7.46              21.24
                   1229.08           7.84              29.08
                   1287.32           8.23              37.32
                   1345.94           8.62              45.94
                   1404.95           9.01              54.95
                   1464.36           9.41              64.36
                   1524.17           9.81              74.17
                   1584.38           10.21             84.38
                   1644.98           10.61             94.98
                   1706             11.01              106


CHANGE DATA AND RECOMPUTE? (1=YES, 0=NO)? 1



PRINCIPAL? 1000
NOMINAL INTEREST RATE? 8
NUMBER OF DEPOSITS/WITHDRAWALS PER YEAR? 4
AMOUNT OF DEPOSIT/WITHDRAWAL? -150
START WITH WHAT YEAR? 1
END PRINTING WITH WHAT YEAR? 1
```

```
              EARNED INTEREST TABLE
  PRINCIPAL $ 1000      AT 8 % NOMINAL     FOR 1 YEARS
REGULAR DEPOSIT/WITHDRAWAL $-150      4  TIMES PER YEAR
          EFFECTIVE INTEREST RATE 8.33 % PER YEAR


YEAR            BALANCE          INTEREST        ACCUM.INTEREST

 1              870.17            20.17            20.17
                737.71            17.54            37.71
                602.58            14.87            52.58
                464.72            12.14            64.72
```

CHANGE DATA AND RECOMPUTE? (1=YES, 0=NO)? 0

END PROGRAM

PROGRAM LISTING

```
   10    PRINT "EARNED INTEREST TABLE"
   20    PRINT
   29    REM - STATEMENTS 30 TO 230 REQUEST USER INPUT
   30    PRINT "PRINCIPAL"; ·
   40    INPUT P
   50    PRINT "NOMINAL INTEREST RATE";
   60    INPUT I
   69    REM - CONVERT PERCENT TO DECIMAL
   70    I=I/100
   80    PRINT  "NUMBER OF DEPOSITS/WITHDRAWALS PER YEAR";
   90    INPUT N1
   99    REM - DON'T ASK FOR AMOUNT IF FREQUENCY IS ZERO
  100    IF N1=0   THEN   160
  108    REM - DEPOSITS ARE·ENTERED AS A POSITIVE NUMBER
  109    REM - WITHDRAWALS ARE ENTERED AS A NEGATIVE NUMBER
  110    PRINT  "AMOUNT OF DEPOSIT/WITHDRAWAL";
  120    INPUT R
  129    REM - INTEREST IS COMPOUNDED DAILY
  130    N=360
  139    REM - PRINT AT EACH DEPOSIT/WITHDRAWAL
  140    L2=N1
  150    GOTO  200
  160    PRINT "NUMBER OF COMPOUNDING PERIODS PER YEAR";
  170    INPUT N
  180    N1=0
  189    REM - PRINT FOUR TIMES PER YEAR
  190    L2=4
  200    PRINT "START WITH WHAT YEAR";
  210    INPUT X
  220    PRINT "END PRINTING WITH WHAT YEAR";
  230    INPUT Y
  239    REM - START PRINTING AT THE BEGINNING OF A YEAR
  240    X=INT(X)
  249    REM - INITIATE RUNNING TOTALS
  250    B0=P
  260    I1=0
  270    I2=0
```

```
280   I3=0
290   K=66
300   P1=4
310   FOR J0=1   TO INT(Y) +1
319   REM - START PRINTING?
320   IF J0<X   THEN   480
329   REM - TEST FOR END OF PAGE
330   IF K<55   THEN   470
339   REM - SPACE TO NEXT PAGE, PRINT HEADINGS (ASSUMED 66 LINES PER PAGE)
340   FOR K1=K   TO 66
350   PRINT
360   NEXT K1
370   K=6
380   PRINT "                         EARNED INTEREST TABLE"
390   PRINT "  PRINCIPAL·$";P;"    AT";I*100;"% NOMINAL    FOR";Y;"YEARS
      "
399   REM - SKIP DEPOSIT/WITHDRAWAL HEADING IF THERE ARE NONE
400   IF N1=0   THEN   430
410   PRINT "REGULAR DEPOSIT/WITHDRAWAL $";R;"  ";N1;" TIMES PER YEAR"
419   REM - K COUNTS THE NUMBER OF PRINTED LINES PER PAGE
420   K=K+1
430   PRINT "             EFFECTIVE INTEREST RATE";FNR(100*((1+I/N)↑N-1));
      "% PER YEAR"
440   PRINT
450   PRINT "YEAR","BALANCE","INTEREST","ACCUM.INTEREST"
459   REM - CALCULATE INTEREST
460   PRINT
469   REM - PRINT YEAR NUMBER
470   PRINT J0,
480   L1=1
490   N2=1
500   P2=1
510   FOR J1=1   TO N
519   REM - DEPOSIT/WITHDRAW ANY MORE THIS YEAR?
520   IF N2>N1   THEN   560
529   REM - TIME TO MAKE DEPOSIT/WITHDRAWAL?
530   IF N2/N1>J1/N   THEN   560
539   REM - CALCULATE NEW BALANCE
540   B0=B0+R
549   REM - COUNT DEPOSITS/WITHDRAWALS MADE PER YEAR
550   N2=N2+1
560   B2=B0*(1+I/N)
569   REM - I1=AMOUNT INTEREST WITH EACH COMPOUNDING PERIOD
570   I1=B2-B0
579   REM - I3=AMOUNT INTEREST ACCUMULATED BETWEEN POSTING
580   I3=I3+I1
589   REM - I2=TOTAL INTEREST ACCUMULATED TO DATE
590   I2=I2+I1
599   REM - ROUND AT INTEREST POSTING TIME
600   IF P2/P1>J1/N   THEN   640
610   I2=FNR(I2)
620   B2=FNR(B2)
630   P2=P2+1
639   REM - YEAR TO START PRINTING?
640   IF J0<X   THEN   710
649   REM - TIME TO PRINT A LINE?
650   IF J1/N<L1/L2   THEN   710
```

```
660    L1=L1+1
670    PRINT FNR(B2),FNR(I3),FNR(I2)
679    REM - INTEREST POSTED, REINITIALIZE INTEREST ACCUM. BETWEEN POSTINGS
680    I3=0
690    K=K+1
699    REM - YEAR NUMBER PRINTED WITH FIRST POSTING IN EACH YEAR ONLY
700    PRINT
710    B0=B2
719    REM - NO MORE LINES TO PRINT IN LAST YEAR?
720    IF J0+J1/N-1>=Y  THEN   780
730    NEXT J1
739    REM - START PRINTING?
740    IF J0<X  THEN   770
750    PRINT
760    K=K+1
770    NEXT J0
780    PRINT
789    REM - RESTART OR END PROGRAM?
790    PRINT "CHANGE DATA AND RECOMPUTE?. (1=YES, 0=NO)";
800    INPUT Z
810    PRINT
820    IF Z=1  THEN   20
829    REM - ROUND OFF FUNCTION
830    DEFFNR(X)=INT(X*100+.5)/100
840    END
```

Depreciation Rate

This program calculates the annual depreciation rate of an investment. You must provide the original price of the item, its resale price, and its age in years.

The depreciation rate is calculated by the following formula:

$$\text{depreciation rate} = 1 - \left(\frac{\text{resale price}}{\text{original price}} \right)^{1/\text{age}}$$

Example:

Joan bought her car for $4933.76 and sold it for $2400.00 three years later. What was its actual depreciation rate?

```
:RUN
DEPRECIATION RATE

ORIGINAL PRICE? 4933.76
RESALE PRICE? 2400
YEARS? 3
DEPRECIATION RATE = 21.354 %

MORE DATA (1=YES, 0=NO)? 0

END PROGRAM
```

```
PROGRAM LISTING

    10   PRINT "DEPRECIATION RATE"
    20   PRINT
    30   PRINT "ORIGINAL PRICE";
    40   INPUT P
    50   PRINT "RESALE PRICE";
    60   INPUT T
    70   PRINT "YEARS";
    80   INPUT Y
    89   REM - CALCULATE DEPRECIATION RATE BY FORMULA, CONVERT TO PERCENT
    90   D=100*(1-(T/P)↑(1/Y))
    99   REM - ROUND OFF, PRINT
   100   PRINT "DEPRECIATION RATE =";INT(1000*D+.5)/1000;"%"
   110   PRINT
   119   REM - RESTART OR END PROGRAM?
   120   PRINT "MORE DATA (1=YES, 0=NO)";
   130   INPUT X
   140   IF X=1  THEN   20
   150   END
```

Depreciation Amount

This program calculates the dollar amount depreciated within a given year for a depreciating investment. You must provide the original price of the investment, its depreciation rate, and the year of depreciation.

The depreciation amount is calculated by the following formula:

$$D = P \cdot i \cdot (1 - i)^{Y-1}$$

where: D =   depreciation amount
           P =   original price
           i =   depreciation rate
           Y =   year of depreciation

Examples:

Joan bought her car for $4933.76. Her model car depreciates at an average annual rate of 21%. What amount has the car depreciated in each of the first three years she has owned it?

Joan is also concerned about the depreciation of the tape deck in her car. It cost her $155.00 two years ago, and has a depreciation rate of 22%. How much will its value decline in year three?

```
:RUN
DEPRECIATION AMOUNT

ORGINAL PRICE? 4933.76
DEPRECIATION RATE? 21
--(ENTER YEAR=0 WHEN NO MORE AMOUNTS DESIRED FOR THIS ITEM)--
YEAR? 1
DEPRECIATION = $ 1036.09

YEAR? 2
DEPRECIATION = $ 818.51

YEAR? 3
DEPRECIATION = $ 646.62

YEAR? 0
MORE DATA (1=YES, 0=NO)? 1

ORGINAL PRICE? 155
DEPRECIATION RATE? 22
--(ENTER YEAR=0 WHEN NO MORE AMOUNTS DESIRED FOR THIS ITEM)--
YEAR? 3
DEPRECIATION = $ 20.75

YEAR? 0
MORE DATA (1=YES, 0=NO)? 0

END PROGRAM
```

```
 10   PRINT "DEPRECIATION AMOUNT"
 20   PRINT
 30   PRINT "ORGINAL PRICE";
 40   INPUT P
 50   PRINT "DEPRECIATION RATE";
 60   INPUT I
 69   REM - CONVERT FROM PERCENT TO DECIMAL
 70   I=I/100
 80   PRINT "--(ENTER YEAR=0 WHEN NO MORE AMOUNTS DESIRED FOR THIS ITEM
      )--"
 90   PRINT "YEAR";
100   INPUT Y
109   REM - THROUGH CALCULATING FOR THIS ITEM?
110   IF Y=0   THEN   160
119   REM - CALCULATE DEPRECIATION AMOUNT BY FORMULA
120   D=P*I*(1-I)↑(Y-1)
129   REM - ROUND OFF TO NEAREST CENT, PRINT
130   PRINT "DEPRECIATION = $";INT(D*100+.5)/100
140   PRINT
149   REM - RETURN FOR NEXT YEAR NUMBER
150   GOTO   90
159   REM - RESTART OR END PROGRAM?
160   PRINT "MORE DATA (1=YES, 0=NO)";
170   INPUT X
180   IF X=1   THEN   20
190   END
```

Salvage Value

This program calculates the salvage value of an item at the end of a given year. It is necessary for you to provide the age of the item, its original price, and its depreciation rate.

The salvage value is obtained by the following formula:

$$S = P(1 - i)^Y$$

where: S = salvage value
P = original price
i = depreciation rate
Y = age in years

Example:

What is the salvage value of Joan's car if it is three years old, she bought it for $4933.76, and it depreciates 21% annually? What would its salvage value be next year?

Joan's tape deck is 2 years old. What is its value if it cost $155.00 originally and depreciates at a rate of 22%?

```
:RUN
SALVAGE VALUE

ORIGINAL PRICE? 4933.76
DEPRECIATION RATE? 21
--(ENTER YEARS=0 WHEN NO MORE VALUES DESIRED FOR THIS ITEM)--
YEARS? 3
VALUE = $ 2432.54

YEARS? 4
VALUE = $ 1921.7

YEARS? 0
MORE DATA (1=YES, 0=NO)? 1

ORIGINAL PRICE? 155
DEPRECIATION RATE? 22
--(ENTER YEARS=0 WHEN NO MORE VALUES DESIRED FOR THIS ITEM)--
YEARS? 2
VALUE = $ 94.3

YEARS? 0
MORE DATA (1=YES, 0=NO)? 0

END PROGRAM


PROGRAM LISTING

10   PRINT "SALVAGE VALUE"
20   PRINT
30   PRINT "ORIGINAL PRICE";
```

```
40    INPUT P
50    PRINT "DEPRECIATION RATE";
60    INPUT I
70    PRINT "--(ENTER YEARS=0 WHEN NO MORE VALUES DESIRED FOR THIS ITEM
    )--"
80    PRINT "YEARS";
90    INPUT Y
99    REM - CALCULATE ANOTHER SALVAGE VALUE?
100   IF Y=0  THEN   140
108   REM - CALCULATE SALVAGE VALUE BY FORMULA, ROUND OFF, PRINT
109   REM - DEPRECIATION RATE CONVERTED TO DECIMAL FOR USE IN CALCULATI
    ONS
110   PRINT "VALUE = $";INT(100*P*(1-I/100)↑Y+.5)/100
120   PRINT
129   REM - RETURN FOR NEXT YEAR NUMBER
130   GOTO   80
139   REM - RESTART OR END PROGRAM?
140   PRINT "MORE DATA (1=YES, 0=NO)";
150   INPUT X
160   IF X=1  THEN   20
170   END
```

Discount Commercial Paper

This program calculates the amount of discount and net cost of a discounted commercial paper. You must provide the future value of the paper, the discount rate and the number of days to maturity.

The formulas used to calculate the discount and cost are as follows:

$$discount = T \cdot \frac{D}{100} \cdot \frac{N}{360}$$

$$cost = T - discount$$

where: T = total future value
D = discount rate
N = number of days to maturity

Example:

Canning Corporation purchases a $625,000.00 commercial paper due in 60 days at 5.4%. What is the discount and cost?

```
:RUN
DISCOUNT COMMERCIAL PAPER

FUTURE VALUE? 625000
DISCOUNT RATE? 5.4
DAYS TO MATURITY? 60
DISCOUNT = $ 5625
    COST = $ 619375

MORE DATA (1=YES, 0-NO)? 0

END PROGRAM
```

PROGRAM LISTING

```
 10   PRINT "DISCOUNT COMMERCIAL PAPER"
 20   PRINT
 29   REM - STATEMENTS 30 TO 90 REQUEST USER INPUT
 30   PRINT "FUTURE VALUE";
 40   INPUT T
 50   PRINT "DISCOUNT RATE";
 60   INPUT D
 69   REM - CONVERT PERCENT TO DECIMAL
 70   D=D/100
 80   PRINT "DAYS TO MATURITY";
 90   INPUT N
 99   REM - CALCULATE DISCOUNT, PRINT
100   D1=T*D*N/360
110   PRINT "DISCOUNT = $";D1
119   REM - CALCULATE COST, PRINT
120   PRINT "    COST = $";T-D1
129   REM - PRINT BLANK LINE TO SEPARATE DATA FROM QUESTION
```

```
130    PRINT
139    REM - RESTART OR END PROGRAM? USER INPUT REQUIRED
140    PRINT "MORE DATA (1=YES, 0-NO)";
150    INPUT X
160    IF X=1   THEN    20
170    END
```

Principal on a Loan

This program calculates an initial amount borrowed. This amount is dependent upon the interest rate, the amount of regular payments, the number of payments per year and the term of the loan.

The calculation is based on the formula:

$$P = \frac{R \cdot N}{i} \cdot \left(1 - \frac{1}{(1 + i/N)^{N \cdot Y}}\right)$$

where:
P = principal
R = regular payment
i = annual interest rate
N = number of payments per year
Y = number of years

Example:

Susan has agreed to pay $250.00 bimonthly for 3 years to repay a loan with 20% interest. What is the amount of the loan?

Tom can afford to make payments of $180.00 per month to repay a loan. If he is willing to make payments for four and a half years and the loan company charges 16% interest, what is the maximum amount Tom can borrow?

```
:RUN
PRINCIPAL ON A LOAN

REGULAR PAYMENT? 250
TERM IN YEARS? 3
ANNUAL INTEREST RATE? 20
NUMBER OF PAYMENTS PER YEAR? 6
PRINCIPAL = $ 3343.45

MORE DATA? (1=YES, 0=NO)? 1

REGULAR PAYMENT? 180
TERM IN YEARS? 4.5
ANNUAL INTEREST RATE? 16
NUMBER OF PAYMENTS PER YEAR? 12
PRINCIPAL = $ 6897.51

MORE DATA? (1=YES, 0=NO)? 0

END PROGRAM


PROGRAM LISTING

 10   PRINT  "PRINCIPAL ON A LOAN"
 20   PRINT
 29   REM - STATEMENTS 30 TO 100 REQUEST USER INPUT
 30   PRINT "REGULAR PAYMENT";
```

```
 40    INPUT R
 50    PRINT   "TERM IN YEARS";
 60    INPUT Y
 70    PRINT   "ANNUAL INTEREST RATE";
 80    INPUT I
 90    PRINT   "NUMBER OF PAYMENTS PER YEAR";
100    INPUT N
108    REM - CALCULATE AMOUNT OF PRINCIPAL BY FORMULA;
109    REM - INTEREST CONVERTED FROM PERCENT TO DECIMAL FOR CALCULATIONS
110    P=R*N*(1-1/((I/100)/N+1)↑(N*Y))/(I/100)
119    REM - ROUND OFF TO NEAREST CENT, PRINT
120    PRINT "PRINCIPAL = $";INT(P*100+.5)/100
129    REM - PRINT BLANK LINE TO SEPARATE DATA FROM QUESTION
130    PRINT
139    REM - RESTART OR END PROGRAM?
140    PRINT   "MORE DATA? (1=YES, 0=NO)";
150    INPUT X
160    IF X=1  THEN   20
170    END
```

OPTION

In some cases it may be more convenient to enter the term of the loan in years and months rather than just years. The program changes necessary are listed following the example below.

Example:

What would be the amount of the mortgage if you were paying $75.00 a month for 11 months with 3% interest?

```
:RUN
PRINCIPAL ON A LOAN

REGULAR PAYMENT? 75
TERM IN YEARS, MONTHS? 0,11
ANNUAL INTEREST RATE? 3
NUMBER OF PAYMENTS PER YEAR? 12
PRINCIPAL = $ 812.76

MORE DATA? (1=YES, 0=NO)? 0

END PROGRAM
```

```
PROGRAM LISTING

  1    REM - OPTION 50-65
 10    PRINT   "PRINCIPAL ON A LOAN"
        ⋮
 40    INPUT R
 50    PRINT   "TERM IN YEARS, MONTHS";
 60    INPUT Y0,M
 64    REM - CALCULATE YEARS FROM YEARS AND MONTHS
 65    Y=(12*Y0+M)/12
 70    PRINT   "ANNUAL INTEREST RATE";
        ⋮
170    END
```

Regular Payment on a Loan

This program calculates the amount required as regular payments in order to repay a loan over a specified time period. The specifications you must provide are the amount of the principal, the interest rate charged, the number of payments to be made per year and the number of years to pay. This program assumes all installment payments will be equal.

The calculation is based on the formula:

$$R = \frac{i \cdot P / N}{1 - \left(\dfrac{i}{N} + 1\right)^{-N \cdot Y}}$$

where: R = regular payment
i = annual interest rate
P = principal
N = number of payments per year
Y = number of years

Examples:

What must you pay on a loan of $4000.00 at 8% if payments are to be made quarterly for five years?

If Michael borrows $6500.00 at 12.5% from Best Rate Savings & Loan to be paid back over a period of 5.5 years, what would his monthly payments be?

```
:RUN
REGULAR PAYMENT ON A LOAN

TERM IN YEARS? 5
PRINCIPAL? 4000
ANNUAL INTEREST RATE? 8
NUMBER OF PAYMENTS PER YEAR? 4
REGULAR PAYMENT = $ 244.63

MORE DATA? (1=YES, 0=NO)? 1

TERM IN YEARS? 5.5
PRINCIPAL? 6500
ANNUAL INTEREST RATE? 12.5
NUMBER OF PAYMENTS PER YEAR? 12
REGULAR PAYMENT = $ 136.68

MORE DATA? (1=YES, 0=NO)? 0

END PROGRAM
```

PROGRAM LISTING

```
10   PRINT "REGULAR PAYMENT ON A LOAN"
20   PRINT
29   REM - STATEMENTS 30 TO 100 REQUEST USER INPUT
```

```
 30    PRINT "TERM IN YEARS";
 40    INPUT Y
 50    PRINT "PRINCIPAL";
 60    INPUT P
 70    PRINT "ANNUAL INTEREST RATE";
 80    INPUT I
 90    PRINT "NUMBER OF PAYMENTS PER YEAR";
100    INPUT N
108    REM - CALCULATE AMOUNT OF REGULAR PAYMENT BY FORMULA;
109    REM - INTEREST CONVERTED FROM PERCENT TO DECIMAL FOR CALCULATIONS
110    R=((I/100)*P/N)/(1-1/((I/100)/N+1)↑(N*Y))
119    REM - ROUND OFF TO NEAREST CENT, PRINT
120    PRINT "REGULAR PAYMENT = $";INT(R*100+.5)/100
129    REM - PRINT BLANK LINE TO SEPARATE DATA FROM QUESTION
130    PRINT
139    REM - RESTART OR END PROGRAM?
140    PRINT "MORE DATA? (1=YES, 0=NO)";
150    INPUT X
160    IF X=1  THEN    20
170    END
```

OPTION

You may find it more convenient to enter the term of payment in years and months rather than years. The program changes necessary are listed following the example below.

Example:

Mr. Terry needs $10,000.00 to put down on a new home. Best Rates offers this amount at 14.0% interest to be repaid over a period of 11 years and 5 months. What would be the amount of regular monthly payments?

```
:RUN
REGULAR PAYMENT ON A LOAN

TERM IN YEARS, MONTHS? 11,5
PRINCIPAL? 10000
ANNUAL INTEREST RATE? 14
NUMBER OF PAYMENTS PER YEAR? 12
REGULAR PAYMENT = $ 146.59

MORE DATA? (1=YES, 0=NO)? 0

END PROGRAM
```

```
PROGRAM LISTING

   1    REM - OPTION 30-45
  10    PRINT "REGULAR PAYMENT ON A LOAN"
         .
         .
  29    REM - STATEMENTS 30 TO 100 REQUEST USER INPUT
  30    PRINT "TERM IN YEARS, MONTHS";
  40    INPUT Y0,M
  44    REM - CALCULATE YEARS FROM YEARS AND MONTHS
  45    Y=(12*Y0+M)/12
  50    PRINT "PRINCIPAL";
         .
         .
 170    END
```

Last Payment on a Loan

This program calculates the amount of the final payment on a loan. This final payment will complete amortization of a loan at the conclusion of its term. You must provide the amount of the loan, the amount of the regular payment, the interest rate charged, the number of payments per year and the term of payment.

The amount of the last payment is normally different from the amount of the regular payment. The final payment will be a "balloon" payment if the final payment is larger than the regular payment. A balloon payment is necessary if applying the amount of the regular payment as the last payment leaves a remaining balance due. In order to entirely pay off the loan at the end of its term, this remaining balance is added to the amount of the regular payment to determine the amount of the last payment.

On the other hand, the amount of the final payment is sometimes less than the regular payment. If the regular payment as the last payment would result in a negative loan balance, then the last payment should be smaller. In this case the regular payment is adjusted by the amount of this hypothetical negative balance to determine the amount of the last payment.

$$\begin{matrix} \text{amount of} \\ \text{last payment} \end{matrix} = \begin{matrix} \text{regular} \\ \text{payment} \end{matrix} + \begin{matrix} \text{hypothetical balance due on a} \\ \text{loan after } N \cdot Y \text{ regular payments} \end{matrix}$$

$$\text{where: } \begin{aligned} N &= \text{number of payments per year} \\ Y &= \text{number of years} \end{aligned}$$

Examples:

Lynn borrowed $6000.00 at 5% from her father for college expenses. If she pays $1000.00 annually for seven years, what will her last payment be?

Lynn borrows $1150.00 at 8% interest to be repaid at a rate of $75.00 per month. A year and two months later Lynn decides to go to Europe. How much must she pay next month to completely pay off her loan?

```
:RUN
LAST PAYMENT ON A LOAN

REGULAR PAYMENT? 1000
PRINCIPAL? 6000
TERM IN YEARS? 7
ANNUAL INTEREST RATE? 5
NUMBER OF PAYMENTS PER YEAR? 1
LAST PAYMENT = $ 1300.59

MORE DATA? (1=YES,0=NO)? 1

REGULAR PAYMENT? 75
PRINCIPAL? 1150
TERM IN YEARS? 1.17
ANNUAL INTEREST RATE? 8
NUMBER OF PAYMENTS PER YEAR? 12
LAST PAYMENT = $ 240.38

MORE DATA? (1=YES,0=NO)? 0

END PROGRAM
```

PROGRAM LISTING

```
10    PRINT   "LAST PAYMENT ON A LOAN"
20    PRINT
29    REM - STATEMENTS 30 TO 130 REQUEST USER INPUT
30    PRINT   "REGULAR PAYMENT";
40    INPUT R
50    PRINT   "PRINCIPAL";
60    INPUT P
70    PRINT   "TERM IN YEARS";
80    INPUT Y
90    PRINT   "ANNUAL INTEREST RATE";
100   INPUT I
109   REM - CONVERT INTEREST FROM PERCENT TO DECIMAL
110   I=I/100
120   PRINT "NUMBER OF PAYMENTS PER YEAR";
130   INPUT N
140   B0=P
149   REM - COMPUTE ALL PAYMENTS, BALANCES THROUGH LAST PAYMENT USING R
150   FOR J1=1  TO N*Y
159   REM - ROUND OFF INTEREST PAID TO NEAREST CENT
160   I1=INT((B0*I/N)*100+.5)/100
169   REM - CALCULATE AMOUNT AMORTIZED WITH EACH PAYMENT
170   A=R-I1
179   REM - BALANCE REMAINING DECREASES WITH EACH PAYMENT
180   B0=B0-A
190   NEXT J1
199   REM - CALCULATE LAST PAYMENT, ROUND OFF, PRINT
200   PRINT "LAST PAYMENT = $" ;INT((R+B0)*100+.5)/100
210   PRINT
219   REM - RESTART OR END PROGRAM?
220   PRINT "MORE DATA? (1=YES,0=NO)";
230   INPUT X
240   IF X=1  THEN    20
250   END
```

OPTION

The program above allows the term of payment on the loan to be entered in years only. You may wish to enter the term in years and months instead. The program changes necessary are listed following the example.

Example:

If you pay $40.00 a month for 2 years and 3 months on a loan of $1200.00 at 7.5%, what amount will the last payment total?

```
:RUN
LAST PAYMENT ON A LOAN

REGULAR PAYMENT? 40
PRINCIPAL? 1200
TERM IN YEARS AND MONTHS? 2,3
ANNUAL INTEREST RATE? 7.5
NUMBER OF PAYMENTS PER YEAR? 12
LAST PAYMENT = $ 287.36

MORE DATA? (1=YES,0=NO)? 0

END PROGRAM
```

```
PROGRAM LISTING

   1   REM - OPTION 70-85
  10   PRINT   "LAST PAYMENT ON A LOAN"
   .
   .
   .
  60   INPUT P
  70   PRINT   "TERM IN YEARS AND MONTHS";
  80   INPUT Y0,M
  84   REM - CALCULATE YEARS FROM YEARS AND MONTHS
  85   Y=(12*Y0+M)/12
  90   PRINT   "ANNUAL INTEREST RATE";
   .
   .
   .
 250   END
```

Remaining Balance on a Loan

This program calculates the balance remaining on a loan after a specified number of payments. It is necessary for you to provide the amount of the regular payment, the number of payments per year, the amount of the principal, the annual interest rate, and the payment number after which to calculate the remaining balance.

The remaining balance is calculated by the following method:

$$\begin{array}{c}\text{remaining} \\ \text{balance}\end{array} = \text{principal} - \begin{array}{c}\text{amount amortized after} \\ N \cdot (Y - 1) + N1 \text{ payments}\end{array}$$

$$\begin{aligned}\text{where:} \quad N &= \text{number of payments per year} \\ Y &= \text{year to calculate remaining balance} \\ N1 &= \text{payment number in year } Y \text{ to calculate remaining balance}\end{aligned}$$

Example:

Kelly has taken out a loan of $8000.00 at 17.2% interest. His regular payments are $200.00 per month. If he has paid through the tenth payment in the fourth year, how much more does Kelly owe on his loan?

```
:RUN
REMAINING BALANCE ON A LOAN

REGULAR PAYMENT? 200
PRINCIPAL? 8000
NUMBER OF PAYMENTS PER YEAR? 12
ANNUAL INTEREST RATE? 17.2
LAST PAYMENT MADE (PAYMENT NO.,YEAR)? 10,4
REMAINING BALANCE = $ 2496.17

MORE DATA? (1=YES,0=NO)? 0

END PROGRAM
```

```
PROGRAM LISTING

  10   PRINT "REMAINING BALANCE ON A LOAN"
  20   PRINT
  29   REM - STATEMENTS 30 TO 130 REQUEST USER INPUT
  30   PRINT "REGULAR PAYMENT";
  40   INPUT R
  50   PRINT "PRINCIPAL";
  60   INPUT P
  70   PRINT "NUMBER OF PAYMENTS PER YEAR";
  80   INPUT N
  90   PRINT "ANNUAL INTEREST RATE";
 100   INPUT I
 109   REM - CONVERT FROM PERCENT TO DECIMAL
 110   I=I/100
 119   REM - ENTER THE PAYMENT NUMBER WITHIN THE YEAR, I.E. N1<=N
 120   PRINT "LAST PAYMENT MADE (PAYMENT NO.,YEAR)";
 130   INPUT N1,Y
 139   REM - INITIALIZE REMAINING BALANCE
 140   B0=P
 149   REM - LOOP TO ACCUMULATE AMOUNT PAID SO FAR
```

```
150    FOR J1=1   TO N*(Y-1)+N1
159    REM - CALCULATE INTEREST PAID WITH EACH PAYMENT
160    I1=INT((B0*I/N)*100+.5)/100
169    REM - CALCULATE AMOUNT AMORTIZED WITH EACH PAYMENT
170    A=R-I1
179    REM - CALCULATE REMAINING BALANCE ON PRINCIPAL
180    B0=B0-A
190    NEXT J1
199    REM - ROUND OFF, PRINT
200    PRINT "REMAINING BALANCE = $";INT(B0*100+.5)/100
210    PRINT
219    REM - RESTART OR END PROGRAM?
220    PRINT "MORE DATA? (1=YES,0=NO)";
230    INPUT X
240    IF X=1   THEN   20
250    END
```

═══

OPTION

You may wish to specify the number of the last payment made as the total payment number rather than the payment number within a certain year. For instance, when 4 payments are made per year, payment 3 of year 3 would be entered as payment number 11. The program changes necessary are listed following the example below.

Example:

John made ten quarterly payments of $550.00 on a loan of $6000.00 with 16% interest. What is his remaining balance?

```
:RUN
REMAINING BALANCE ON A LOAN

REGULAR PAYMENT? 550
PRINCIPAL? 6000
NUMBER OF PAYMENTS PER YEAR? 4
ANNUAL INTEREST RATE? 16
NUMBER OF PAYMENTS MADE? 10
REMAINING BALANCE = $ 2278.09

MORE DATA? (1=YES,0=NO)? 0

END PROGRAM
```

```
PROGRAM LISTING

   1   REM - OPTION 119-130, 150
  10   PRINT "REMAINING BALANCE ON A LOAN"
   .
   .
 110   I=I/100
 119   REM - ENTER THE TOTAL NUMBER OF PAYMENTS MADE TO DATE
 120   PRINT "NUMBER OF PAYMENTS MADE";
 130   INPUT N1
 139   REM - INITIALIZE REMAINING BALANCE
 140   B0=P
 149   REM - LOOP TO ACCUMULATE AMOUNT PAID SO FAR
 150   FOR J1=1   TO N1
 159   REM - CALCULATE INTEREST PAID WITH EACH PAYMENT
   .
   .
 250   END
```

Term of a Loan

This program calculates the period of time needed to repay a loan. You must specify the amount of the loan, the amount of the payments, the number of payments to be made per year and the annual interest rate on the loan. All payments are assumed to be equal.

The term of payment is derived from the following formula:

$$Y = -\frac{\log\left(1 - \dfrac{P \cdot i}{N \cdot R}\right)}{\log\left(1 + \dfrac{i}{N}\right)} \cdot \frac{1}{N}$$

where:
- Y = term of payment in years
- P = principal
- i = annual interest rate
- N = number of payments per year
- R = amount of payments

Examples:

What would be the duration of payment on a mortgage of $20,000.00 at 18% when payments of $1000.00 are to be made quarterly?

Sally takes out a loan for $12,669.00 at 16.8%. Her payments are $512.34 every two months. What is the term of her loan?

```
:RUN
TERM OF A LOAN

REGULAR PAYMENT? 1000
PRINCIPAL? 20000
ANNUAL INTEREST RATE? 18
NUMBER OF PAYMENTS PER YEAR? 4
TERM = 13.1 YEARS

MORE DATA? (1=YES, 0=NO)? 1

REGULAR PAYMENT? 512.34
PRINCIPAL? 12669
ANNUAL INTEREST RATE? 16.8
NUMBER OF PAYMENTS PER YEAR? 6
TERM = 7.1 YEARS

MORE DATA? (1=YES, 0=NO)? 0

END PROGRAM
```

PROGRAM LISTING

```
10    PRINT "TERM OF A LOAN"
20    PRINT
29    REM - STATEMENTS 30 TO 100 REQUEST USER INPUT
30    PRINT "REGULAR PAYMENT";
40    INPUT R
50    PRINT "PRINCIPAL";
60    INPUT P
70    PRINT "ANNUAL INTEREST RATE";
80    INPUT I
90    PRINT "NUMBER OF PAYMENTS PER YEAR";
100   INPUT N
108   REM - CALCULATE TERM IN YEARS BY FORMULA;
109   REM - INTEREST CONVERTED FROM PERCENT TO DECIMAL FOR CALCULATION
110   Y=-(LOG(1-(P*(I/100))/(N*R))/(LOG(1+I/100/N)*N))
119   REM - ROUND OFF TO NEAREST TENTH, PRINT
120   PRINT "TERM =";INT(Y*10+.5)/10;"YEARS"
130   PRINT
139   REM - RESTART OR END PROGRAM?
140   PRINT "MORE DATA? (1=YES, 0=NO)";
150   INPUT X
160   IF X=1  THEN   20
170   END
```

OPTION

It is possible to calculate the term of payment in years and months rather than just years. To do this, make the program changes listed following the example below.

Example:

Dick took out a loan for $8000.00 at 7.5%. Regular payments of $150.00 are to be made monthly. How long will it take to pay off the loan?

```
:RUN
TERM OF A LOAN

REGULAR PAYMENT? 150
PRINCIPAL? 8000
ANNUAL INTEREST RATE? 7.5
NUMBER OF PAYMENTS PER YEAR? 12
TERM = 5 YEARS, 5 MONTHS

MORE DATA? (1=YES, 0=NO)? 0

END PROGRAM
```

```
PROGRAM LISTING

    1    REM - OPTION 114-120
   10    PRINT "TERM OF A LOAN"
    .
    .
  110    Y=-(LOG(1-(P*(I/100))/(N*R))/(LOG(1+I/100/N)*N))
  114    REM - CALCULATE YEARS AND MONTHS FROM YEARS
  115    M=INT(Y*12+.5)
  116    Y0=INT(M/12)
  117    M=M-Y0*12
  119    REM - PRINT RESULTS
  120    PRINT "TERM =";Y0;"YEARS,";M;"MONTHS"
  130    PRINT
    .
    .
  170    END
```

Annual Interest Rate on a Loan

This program calculates the rate at which interest is charged on a loan. To determine this rate you must enter the amount of the loan, the amount of the regular payment, the number of payments per year, and the term of the loan.

The annual interest rate is computed by the following method of approximation:

1) Guess an interest rate
   Initialize last guess to 0

2) Compute regular payment using guessed rate:

$$R_1 = \frac{i \cdot P/N}{1 - (1 + i/N)^{-N \cdot Y}}$$

   Round off R_1

3) If computed payment = actual payment, then current guess = approximate interest rate

4) Otherwise, save current guess and calculate a new guess

$$i_2 = i$$

$$i = i \pm |(i - i_2)/2| \begin{cases} + \text{ if } R_1 < R \\ - \text{ if } R_1 > R \end{cases}$$

5) Go to 2

where:
i = interest rate
i_2 = previous interest rate
R = input regular payment
R_1 = computed regular payment
P = principal
N = number of payments per year
Y = number of years

Examples:

Cindy borrowed $3000.00 from her friend George with an agreement to pay back $400.00 quarterly for 2 years. At what interest rate is she being charged?

To pay back a loan of $10,000.00 John contracted to make monthly payments of $120.00 for 9.5 years. At what rate is interest being charged?

```
:RUN
ANNUAL INTEREST RATE ON A LOAN

REGULAR PAYMENT? 400
TERM IN YEARS? 2
PRINCIPAL? 3000
NUMBER OF PAYMENTS PER YEAR? 4
ANNUAL INTEREST RATE = 5.827 %

MORE DATA? (1=YES, 0=NO)? 1

REGULAR PAYMENT? 120
TERM IN YEARS? 9.5
PRINCIPAL? 10000
NUMBER OF PAYMENTS PER YEAR? 12
ANNUAL INTEREST RATE = 6.933 %

MORE DATA? (1=YES, 0=NO)? 0

END PROGRAM
```

41

```
10    PRINT   "AN   AL INTEREST RATE ON A LOAN"
20    PRINT
29    REM - STATEMENTS 30 TO 100 REQUEST USER INPUT
30    PRINT "REGULAR PAYMENT";
40    INPUT R
50    PRINT "TERM IN YEARS";
60    INPUT Y
70    PRINT "PRINCIPAL";
80    INPUT P
90    PRINT   "NUMBER OF PAYMENTS PER YEAR";
100   INPUT N
109   REM - GUESS AN INTEREST RATE (10%) TO INITIATE TESTING
110   I=10
119   REM - I2=LAST GUESS OR ESTIMATE (START WITH 0)
120   I2=0
129   REM - COMPUTE REGULAR PAYMENT USING GUESSED INTEREST RATE
130   R1=(I*P/N)/(1-1/((I/N+1)↑(N*Y)))
139   REM - ROUND OFF TO NEAREST CENT
140   R1=INT(R1*100+.5)/100
149   REM - I3=NUMBER USED TO CLOSE IN ON INTEREST RATE
150   I3=ABS(I-I2)/2
159   REM - SAVE THIS GUESS
160   I2=I
168   REM - COMPARE COMPUTED PAYMENT (R1) TO INPUT PAYMENT (R);
169   REM - IF THEY'RE EQUAL, LAST RATE GUESSED=APPROXIMATE INT. RATE
170   IF R1=R    THEN   230
180   IF R1>R    THEN   210
189   REM - R1<R, RATE MUST BE HIGHER THAN LAST GUESS
190   I=I+I3
199   REM - RETEST WITH NEW GUESS
200   GOTO  130
209   REM - R1>R, RATE MUST BE LOWER THAN LAST GUESS
210   I=I-I3
219   REM - RETEST WITH NEW GUESS
220   GOTO  130
229   REM - COMPUTE INTEREST TO PROPER PROPORTIONS, ROUND OFF, PRINT
230   I=((INT((I*1000)*100+.5))/100)/1000
240   PRINT "ANNUAL INTEREST RATE =";I*100;"%"
250   PRINT
259   REM - RESTART OR END PROGRAM?
260   PRINT "MORE DATA? (1=YES, 0=NO)";
270   INPUT X
280   IF X=1   THEN   20
290   END
```

OPTION

The above listing allows the term of the loan to be entered in years only. You may wish to enter the term in years and months rather than years. The program changes necessary are listed following the example below.

Example:

If Connie pays $100.00 per month for 11 years and 7 months on a $10,000.00 loan, what is the annual interest rate on the loan?

```
:RUN
ANNUAL INTEREST RATE ON A LOAN

REGULAR PAYMENT? 100
TERM IN YEARS, MONTHS? 11,7
PRINCIPAL? 10000
NUMBER OF PAYMENTS PER YEAR? 12
ANNUAL INTEREST RATE = 6.002 %

MORE DATA? (1=YES, 0=NO)? 0

END PROGRAM
```

PROGRAM LISTING

```
    1   REM - OPTION 50-65
   10   PRINT  "ANNUAL INTEREST RATE ON A. LOAN"
    .
    .
   40   INPUT R
   50   PRINT "TERM IN YEARS, MONTHS";
   60   INPUT Y0,M
   64   REM - CALCULATE YEARS FROM YEARS AND MONTHS
   65   Y=(12*Y0+M)/12
   70   PRINT "PRINCIPAL";
    .
    .
  290   END
```

Mortgage Amortization Table

This program calculates and prints a loan repayment schedule. This schedule provides the following outputs:

1) Payment number
2) Amount of each payment paid as interest
3) Amount of the loan amortized with each payment
4) Balance remaining on the principal at the time of each payment
5) Accumulated interest paid at the time of each payment
6) Amount of the last payment

In addition, the yearly totals of interest paid and amount amortized are tabulated and printed.

To use this program you must supply the amount of the regular payment, the term of payment, the number of payments per year, the amount of the principal and the annual interest rate.

The schedule is calculated in the following manner:

1) Payment number = payment number within each year
2) Amount of each payment paid as interest = remaining balance $\cdot i/N$
   where: i = annual interest rate
   N = number of payments per year
3) Amount amortized with each payment = $R - I$
   where: R = amount of regular payment
   I = amount of each payment paid as interest
4) Balance remaining = $P - \Sigma A$
   where: P = principal
   ΣA = sum of amounts amortized with each payment to date
5) Accumulated interest = ΣI
   where: ΣI = sum of amounts of each payment paid as interest to date
6) Amount of last payment = $R + (P - R \cdot N \cdot Y)$
   where: R = regular payment
   P = principal
   N = number of payments per year
   Y = number of years

Example:

David needs $2100.00 to pay off some debts. His sister offers him the money at 6% interest. With payments of $75.00 monthly for 2½ years, what is David's repayment schedule?

```
:RUN
MORTGAGE AMORTIZATION TABLE

REGULAR PAYMENT? 75
TERM IN YEARS? 2.5
PRINCIPAL? 2100
ANNUAL INTEREST RATE? 6
NUMBER OF PAYMENTS PER YEAR? 12
START PRINTING WITH WHAT YEAR? 1
```

```
                    MORTGAGE AMORTIZATION TABLE
        PRINCIPAL $ 2100      AT 5 %    FOR 2.5 YEARS
                    REGULAR PAYMENT = $ 75

NO.     INTEREST   AMORTIZED       BALANCE          ACCUM INTEREST
 1       10.5       64.5           2035.5            10.5
 2       10.18      64.82          1970.68           20.68
 3        9.85      65.15          1905.53           30.53
 4        9.53      65.47          1840.06           40.06
 5        9.2       65.8           1774.26           49.26
 6        8.87      66.13          1708.13           58.13
 7        8.54      66.46          1641.67           66.67
 8        8.21      66.79          1574.88           74.88
 9        7.87      67.13          1507.75           82.75
10        7.54      67.46          1440.29           90.29
11        7.2       67.8           1372.49           97.49
12        6.86      68.14          1304.35          104.35

YR. 1   104.35     795.65

 1        6.52      68.48          1235.87          110.87
 2        6.18      68.82          1167.05          117.05
 3        5.84      69.16          1097.89          122.89
 4        5.49      69.51          1028.38          128.38
 5        5.14      69.86           958.52          133.52
 6        4.79      70.21           888.31          138.31
 7        4.44      70.56           817.75          142.75
 8        4.09      70.91           746.84          146.84
 9        3.73      71.27           675.57          150.57
10        3.38      71.62           603.95          153.95
11        3.02      71.98           531.97          156.97
12        2.66      72.34           459.63          159.63

YR. 2    55.28     844.72

 1        2.3       72.7            386.93          161.93
 2        1.93      73.07           313.86          163.86
 3        1.57      73.43           240.43          165.43
 4        1.2       73.8            166.63          166.63
 5         .83      74.17            92.46          167.46
 6         .46      92.46             0             167.92
         LAST PAYMENT = $ 92.92

YR. 3     8.29     459.63


CHANGE DATA AND RECOMPUTE?  (1=YES,  0=NO)? 0

END PROGRAM


PROGRAM LISTING

   10   PRINT "MORTGAGE AMORTIZATION TABLE"
   20   PRINT
   29   REM - STATEMENTS 30 TO 150 REQUEST USER INPUT
   30   PRINT "REGULAR PAYMENT";
   40   INPUT R
```

```
50    PRINT "TERM IN YEARS";
60    INPUT Y
70    PRINT "PRINCIPAL";
80    INPUT P
90    PRINT "ANNUAL INTEREST RATE";
100   INPUT I
109   REM - CONVERT FROM PERCENT TO DECIMAL
110   I=I/100
120   PRINT "NUMBER OF PAYMENTS PER YEAR";
130   INPUT N
140   PRINT  "START PRINTING WITH WHAT YEAR";
150   INPUT X
159   REM - START PRINTING AT BEGINNING OF A YEAR
160   X=INT(X)
169   REM - INITIALIZE VARIABLES
170   C1=0
180   I2=0
190   I3=0
200   J0=0
210   N1=N
220   K=66
230   B0=P
240   A1=0
250   A2=0
259   REM - TERM LESS THAN ONE YEAR?
260   IF INT(Y)>=1  THEN  270
261   REM - ADJUST VARIABLES TO PRINT A PARTIAL YEAR
262   N1=((Y-INT(Y))*12)/12*N
263   J0=J0+1
264   GOTO  280
269   REM - LOOP FOR EACH YEAR
270   FOR J0=1  TO INT(Y)
279   REM - START PRINTING?
280   IF J0<X  THEN  410
289   REM - NEED TO START NEXT PAGE?
290   IF K+N+3<58  THEN  400
299   REM - SPACE TO TOP OF NEXT PAGE (ASSUME 66 LINES PER PAGE)
300   FOR K1=K  TO 66
310   PRINT
320   NEXT K1
330   PRINT
339   REM - PRINT PAGE HEADINGS
340   PRINT  "                    MORTGAGE AMORTIZATION TABLE"
350   PRINT  "      PRINCIPAL $";P;"     AT";I*100;"%     FOR";Y; "YEARS"
360   PRINT  "                         REGULAR PAYMENT = $";R
370   PRINT
380   PRINT  "NO.   ";"INTEREST","AMORTIZED","BALANCE","ACCUM INTEREST"
389   REM - COUNT LINES PRINTED ON EACH PAGE IN K
390   K=7
400   K=K+N+3
410   FOR J1=1  TO N1
419   REM - CALCULATE INTEREST PAID THIS PAYMENT, ROUND OFF
420   I1=INT((B0*I/N)*100+.5)/100
429   REM - COUNT NUMBER OF PAYMENTS MADE SO FAR
430   C1=C1+1
439   REM - CALCULATE AMOUNT AMORTIZED THIS PAYMENT
440   A=R-I1
```

```
449   REM - SUM AMOUNT AMORTIZED TO DATE
450   A1=A1+A
459   REM - CALCULATE BALANCE DUE
460   B0=P-A1
468   REM - LAST PAYMENT? IF YES, CALCULATE AMOUNT SO THAT THE
469   REM - BALANCE DUE EQUALS $00.00 AFTER THIS PAYMENT
470   IF C1<>N*Y   THEN   520
480   R=R+B0
490   A=A+B0
500   A1=A1+B0
510   B0=0
519   REM - SUM INTEREST PAID TO DATE
520   I2=I2+I1
529   REM - SUM INTEREST PAID THIS YEAR
530   I3=I3+I1
539   REM - SUM AMOUNT AMORTIZED THIS YEAR
540   A2=A2+A
549   REM - STARTED PRINTING? IF YES, PRINT COMPUTED VALUES IN TABLE
550   IF J0<X   THEN   570
560   PRINT J1;"     ";I1,A,B0,I2
570   NEXT J1
579   REM - LAST PAYMENT? IF YES, ROUND OFF, PRINT
580   IF C1<>N*Y   THEN   600
590   PRINT   "         LAST PAYMENT = $";(INT(R*100+.5))/100
599   REM - STARTED PRINTING? IF YES, PRINT YEARLY TOTALS
600   IF J0<X   THEN   640
610   PRINT
620   PRINT "YR.";J0;I3,A2
630   PRINT
639   REM - COMPLETED TERM?
640   IF J0>Y   THEN   720
649   REM - REINITIALIZE YEARLY VARIABLES
650   I3=0
660   A2=0
670   NEXT J0
679   REM - NEED TO PRINT A PARTIAL YEAR?
680   IF Y<>J0   THEN   262
720   PRINT
729   REM - RESTART OR END PROGRAM?
730   PRINT "CHANGE DATA AND RECOMPUTE? (1=YES, 0=NO)";
740   INPUT Z
750   IF Z=1   THEN   20
760   END
```

OPTION

You may wish to enter the term of payment in years and months rather than years. The program changes necessary are listed following the example below.

Example:

If you took out a loan for $700.00 from a friend at 9% interest and were to pay $100.00 per month for 8 months, what would your repayment schedule be?

```
:RUN
MORTGAGE AMORTIZATION TABLE

REGULAR PAYMENT? 100
TERM IN YEARS, MONTHS? 0,8
PRINCIPAL? 700
ANNUAL INTEREST RATE? 9
NUMBER OF PAYMENTS PER YEAR? 12
START PRINTING WITH WHAT YEAR? 1


                    MORTGAGE AMORTIZATION TABLE
    PRINCIPAL $ 700     AT 9 %   FOR 0 YEARS 8 MONTHS
                    REGULAR PAYMENT = $ 100

NO.   INTEREST   AMORTIZED        BALANCE        ACCUM INTEREST
 1     5.25       94.75           605.25          5.25
 2     4.54       95.46           509.79          9.79
 3     3.82       96.18           413.61          13.61
 4     3.1        96.9            316.71          16.71
 5     2.38       97.62           219.09          19.09
 6     1.64       98.36           120.73          20.73
 7     .91        99.09           21.64           21.64
 8     .16        21.64           0               21.8
        LAST PAYMENT = $ 21.8

YR. 1  21.8        700


CHANGE DATA AND RECOMPUTE? (1=YES, 0=NO)? 0

END PROGRAM


PROGRAM LISTING

    1   REM - OPTION 50-65,350
   10   PRINT "MORTGAGE AMORTIZATION TABLE"
     .
     .
   40   INPUT R
   50   PRINT "TERM IN YEARS, MONTHS";
   60   INPUT Y0,M
   64   REM - CONVERT YEARS AND MONTHS TO YEARS
   65   Y=(12*Y0+M)/12
   70   PRINT "PRINCIPAL";
     .
     .
  340   PRINT "              MORTGAGE AMORTIZATION TABLE"
  350   PRINT " PRINCIPAL $";P;"    AT";I*100;"%    FOR";Y0;"YEARS";M;"MONT
      HS"
  360   PRINT "              REGULAR PAYMENT = $";R
     .
     .
  760   END
```

Greatest Common Denominator

This program calculates the greatest common denominator of two integers. It is based on the Euclidean algorithm for finding the GCD:

1) Enter A, B
   A = absolute value of A
   B = absolute value of B

2) Calculate $R = A - B \cdot$ (integer of (A/B))

3) Is $R = 0$?. If yes, the GCD $= B$
   If no, go to step 4

4) $A = B$
   $B = R$

5) Go to step 2

Example:

Find the greatest common denominator of 50 and 18, 115 and 150.

```
:RUN
GREATEST COMMON DENOMINATOR

(ENTER 0,0 TO END PROGRAM)
ENTER TWO NUMBERS? 50,18
G.C.D: 2

ENTER TWO NUMBERS? 115,150
G.C.D: 5

ENTER TWO NUMBERS? 0,0

END PROGRAM
```

```
PROGRAM LISTING

   10   PRINT "GREATEST COMMON DENOMINATOR"
   20   PRINT
   30   PRINT "(ENTER 0,0 TO END PROGRAM)"
   40   PRINT "ENTER TWO NUMBERS";
   50   INPUT A,B
   59   REM - END PROGRAM?
   60   IF A<>0  THEN    90
   70   IF B<>0  THEN    90
   80   GOTO  190
   89   REM - CALCULATE GCD ACCORDING TO EUCLIDEAN ALGORITHM, PRINT RESULT
   90   A=ABS(A)
  100   B=ABS(B)
  110   R=A-B*INT(A/B)
  120   IF R=0  THEN   160
  130   A=B
  140   B=R
```

```
150    GOTO   110
160    PRINT "G.C.D:";B
169    REM - PRINT BLANK LINE TO SEPARATE SETS OF DATA
170    PRINT
179    REM - RESTART PROGRAM
180    GOTO    40
190    END
```

Prime Factors of Integers

This program lists the prime factors of an integer. It will not test for the integer 0.

Examples:

What are the prime factors of -49?

Factor 92 into primes.

```
:RUN
PRIME FACTORS OF INTEGERS

(ENTER 0 TO END PROGRAM)
NUMBER? -49
-1
 7 ↑ 2
NUMBER? 92
 1
 2 ↑ 2
 23 ↑ 1
NUMBER? 0
END PROGRAM
```

PROGRAM LISTING

```
10    PRINT "PRIME FACTORS OF INTEGERS"
20    PRINT
30    PRINT "(ENTER 0 TO END PROGRAM)"
40    PRINT "NUMBER";
50    INPUT Z
59    REM - END PROGRAM?
60    IF Z=0  THEN  200
69    REM - THE SIGN OF THE NUMBER IS ALWAYS A FACTOR
70    PRINT SGN(Z)
79    REM - USE ABSOLUTE VALUE FOR CALCULATIONS
80    Z=ABS(Z)
88    REM - LOOP TO TEST ALL INTEGERS (2 THROUGH Z) AS PRIME FACTORS
89    REM - INTEGERS SQR(Z) THRU Z WILL HAVE NO NEW FACTORS
90    FOR I=2  TO SQR(Z)
100   S=0
110   IF Z/I<>INT(Z/I)  THEN  150
120   Z=Z/I
130   S=S+1
140   GOTO  110
149   REM - FIND A PRIME FACTOR? IF YES, PRINT
150   IF S=0  THEN  170
159   REM - PRINT FACTORS WITH EXPONENTS; I↑S = I TO THE S POWER
160   PRINT I;"↑";S
170   NEXT I
180   PRINT
189   REM - RESTART PROGRAM
190   GOTO   40
200   END
```

Area of a Polygon

This program calculates the area of a polygon. You must supply the x- and y-coordinates of all vertices. Coordinates must be entered in order of successive vertices.

The formula used to calculate the area is:

$$\text{Area} = (x_1 + x_2) \cdot (y_1 - y_2) + (x_2 + x_3) \cdot (y_2 - y_3) + \ldots (x_n + x_1) \cdot (y_n - y_1) \, 12$$

where $n =$ the number of vertices.

The number of vertices you may enter is currently limited to 24. You may increase or decrease this limit by altering statement 30 according to the following scheme:

```
30 DIM X(n+1), Y(n+1)
```

Example:

Approximate the area of Lake Boyer.

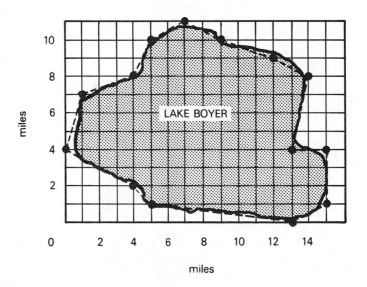

```
:RUN
AREA OF A POLYGON

NUMBER OF VERTICES (ENTER 0 TO END PROGRAM)? 14
COORDINATES OF VERTEX 1 ? 0,4
              VERTEX 2 ? 1,7
              VERTEX 3 ? 4,8
              VERTEX 4 ? 5,10
              VERTEX 5 ? 7,11
              VERTEX 6 ? 9,10
              VERTEX 7 ? 12,9
```

```
                    VERTEX 8 ? 14,8
                    VERTEX 9 ? 13,4
                    VERTEX 10 ? 15,4
                    VERTEX 11 ? 15,1
                    VERTEX 12 ? 13,0
                    VERTEX 13 ? 5,1
                    VERTEX 14 ? 4,2
AREA = 108

NUMBER OF VERTICES (ENTER 0 TO END PROGRAM)? 0

END PROGRAM


PROGRAM LISTING

  10    PRINT "AREA OF A POLYGON"
  20    PRINT
  29    REM - COORDINATE ARRAYS SHOULD BE SET TO (NUMBER OF VERTICES +1)
  30    DIM X(25),Y(25)
  40    PRINT "NUMBER OF VERTICES (ENTER 0 TO END PROGRAM)";
  50    INPUT N
  59    REM - END PROGRAM?
  60    IF N=0  THEN   230
  69    REM - LOOP TO ENTER COORDINATES IN ORDER OF SUCCESSIVE VERTICES
  70    FOR I=1  TO N
  80    IF I>1  THEN   110
  90    PRINT "COORDINATES OF VERTEX";I;
 100    GOTO  120
 110    PRINT "                    VERTEX";I;
 120    INPUT X(I),Y(I)
 130    NEXT I
 139    REM - FIRST VERTEX SERVES AS LAST VERTEX
 140    X(N+1)=X(1)
 150    Y(N+1)=Y(1)
 160    A=0
 169    REM - CALCULATE AREA, PRINT
 170    FOR I=1  TO N
 180    A=A+(X(I)+X(I+1))*(Y(I)-Y(I+1))
 190    NEXT I
 200    PRINT "AREA =";ABS(A)/2
 210    PRINT
 219    REM - RESTART PROGRAM
 220    GOTO   40
 230    END
```

Parts of a Triangle

This program calculates three unknown parts of a triangle when three parts are given. At least one part given must be the length of a side. There are five possibilities for data entry:

1) Angle, side, angle
2) Side, angle, side
3) Angle, angle, side
4) Side, side, angle
5) Side, side, side

Data must be entered in the order it appears in a triangle, either clockwise or counterclockwise.

Example:

The base of a triangle measures 14 inches. The base angles measure .45 and 2.1 radians. What are the measurements of the triangle?

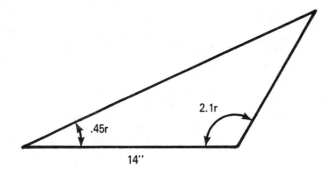

```
:RUN
PARTS OF A TRIANGLE

PROBLEM TYPES: 1=ASA,2=SAS,3=AAS,4=SSA,5=SSS,6=END PROGRAM
ENTER PROBLEM TYPE? 1
ENTER ANGLE,SIDE,ANGLE? .45,14,2.1

SIDE 1 = 10.919
OPPOSITE ANGLE= .45 RADIANS
SIDE 2 = 21.67
OPPOSITE ANGLE= 2.1 RADIANS
SIDE 3 = 14
OPPOSITE ANGLE= .592 RADIANS

ENTER PROBLEM TYPE? 6

END PROGRAM
```

```
10    PRINT "PARTS OF A TRIANGLE"
20    PRINT
30    DIM A(3),S(3)
31    REM - SET VALUE OF PI
40    P=3.1415927
48    REM - ENTER NUMBER OF PROBLEM TYPE ACCORDING TO KNOWN PARTS
49    REM - OF THE TRIANGLE WHERE A=ANGLE, S=LENGTH OF SIDE
50    PRINT "PROBLEM TYPES: 1=ASA,2=SAS,3=AAS,4=SSA,5=SSS,6=END PROGRAM
      "
60    PRINT "ENTER PROBLEM TYPE";
70    INPUT X
79    REM - DIRECT PROGRAM TO PROPER CALCULATIONS
80    IF X=6   THEN   560
90    IF X=5   THEN   390
100   IF X=4   THEN   300
110   IF X=3   THEN   260
120   IF X=2   THEN   190
130   PRINT "ENTER ANGLE,SIDE,ANGLE";
140   INPUT A(1),S(3),A(2)
150   A(3)=P-A(1)-A(2)
160   S(1)=S(3)*SIN(A(1))/SIN(A(3))
170   S(2)=S(3)*SIN(A(2))/SIN(A(3))
180   GOTO   440
190   PRINT "ENTER SIDE,ANGLE,SIDE";
200   INPUT S(3),A(1),S(2)
210   S(1)=SQR(S(3)↑2+S(2)↑2-2*S(3)*S(2)*COS(A(1)))
220   A(2)=SIN(A(1))/S(1)*S(2)
230   A(2)=ARCSIN(A(2))
240   A(3)=P-A(1)-A(2)
250   GOTO   440
260   PRINT "ENTER ANGLE,ANGLE,SIDE";
270   INPUT A(3),A(2),S(3)
280   A(1)=P-A(2)-A(3)
290   GOTO   160
300   PRINT "ENTER SIDE,SIDE,ANGLE";
310   INPUT S(1),S(2),A(1)
320   T=S(2)*SIN(A(1))
330   IF S(1)<T   THEN   520
340   S(3)=SQR(S(2)↑2-T↑2)
350   IF S(1)<=T   THEN   380
360   Y=SQR(S(1)↑2-T↑2)
370   S(3)=S(3)+Y
380   GOTO   220
390   PRINT "ENTER SIDE,SIDE,SIDE";
400   INPUT S(1),S(2),S(3)
410   A(1)=(S(2)↑2+S(3)↑2-S(1)↑2)/2/S(2)/S(3)
420   A(1)=ARCCOS(A(1))
430   GOTO   220
440   PRINT
449   REM - PRINT RESULTS
450   FOR I=1   TO 3
459   REM - THE ANGLE OF A TRIANGLE CANNOT BE LESS THAN ZERO
460   IF A(I)<0   THEN   520
470   PRINT "SIDE";I;"=";INT(S(I)*1000+.5)/1000
480   PRINT "OPPOSITE ANGLE=";INT(A(I)*1000+.5)/1000;"RADIANS"
```

```
490    NEXT I
500    PRINT
510    GOTO    60
520    PRINT
530    PRINT  "NO SOLUTION"
540    PRINT
550    GOTO    60
560    END
```

OPTION

It may be more convenient for you to work with angles in degrees rather than radians. The program changes necessary are listed following the examples below.

Examples:

A square measures 8.76″ x 8.76″. What is the length of its diagonal?

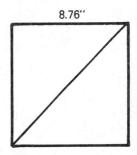

The ladder of a slide measures 10′, the slide 14′, and it covers 13′ of ground from base of ladder to tip of slide. How steep is the slide?

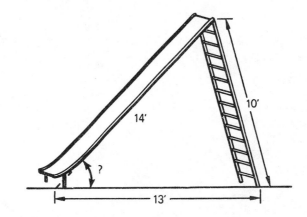

```
:RUN
PARTS OF A TRIANGLE

PROBLEM TYPES: 1=ASA,2=SAS,3=AAS,4=SSA,5=SSS,6=END PROGRAM
ENTER PROBLEM TYPE? 2
ENTER SIDE,ANGLE,SIDE? 8.76,90,8.76

SIDE 1 = 12.389
OPPOSITE ANGLE= 90 DEGREES
SIDE 2 = 8.76
OPPOSITE ANGLE= 45 DEGREES
SIDE 3 = 8.76
OPPOSITE ANGLE= 45 DEGREES
```

```
ENTER PROBLEM TYPE? 5
ENTER SIDE,SIDE,SIDE? 10,13,14

SIDE 1 = 10
OPPOSITE ANGLE= 43.279 DEGREES
SIDE 2 = 13
OPPOSITE ANGLE= 63.027 DEGREES
SIDE 3 = 14
OPPOSITE ANGLE= 73.694 DEGREES

ENTER PROBLEM TYPE? 6

END PROGRAM
```

PROGRAM LISTING

```
   1    REM - OPTION 44-45,145-146,205,275-276,305,480
  10    PRINT "PARTS OF A TRIANGLE"
   ⋮
  40    P=3.1415927
  44    REM - SET CONVERSION FACTOR FOR CONVERTING DEGREES TO RADIANS
  45    C=.0174532927
  48    REM - ENTER NUMBER OF PROBLEM TYPE ACCORDING TO KNOWN PARTS
   ⋮
 140    INPUT A(1),S(3),A(2)
 145    A(1)=A(1)*C
 146    A(2)=A(2)*C
 150    A(3)=P-A(1)-A(2)
   ⋮
 200    INPUT S(3),A(1),S(2)
 205    A(1)=A(1)*C
 210    S(1)=SQR(S(3)↑2+S(2)↑2-2*S(3)*S(2)*COS(A(1)))
   ⋮
 270    INPUT A(3),A(2),S(3)
 275    A(3)=A(3)*C
 276    A(2)=A(2)*C
 280    A(1)=P-A(2)-A(3)
   ⋮
 310    INPUT S(1),S(2),A(1)
 315    A(1)=A(1)*C
 320    T=S(2)*SIN(A(1))
   ⋮
 470    PRINT "SIDE";I;"=";INT(S(I)*1000+.5)/1000
 480    PRINT "OPPOSITE ANGLE=";INT(A(I)/C*1000+.5)/1000;"DEGREES"
 490    NEXT I
   ⋮
 560    END
```

Analysis of Two Vectors

This program calculates the angle between two given vectors, the angle between each vector and axis, and the magnitude of each vector. The vectors are given in three dimensional space.

Example:

Find the angle (θ) between a diagonal of a cube and a diagonal of one of its faces. The cube measures 4 x 4 x 4.

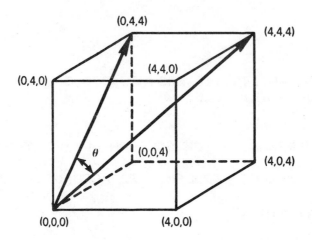

```
:RUN
ANALYSIS OF TWO VECTORS

VECTOR 1: X,Y,Z? 0,4,4
VECTOR 2: X,Y,Z? 4,4,4

VECTOR 1 :
MAGNITUDE: 5.6568542495
ANGLE WITH X-AXIS: 90.00000076485
ANGLE WITH Y-AXIS: 45.00000033257
ANGLE WITH Z-AXIS: 45.00000038257

VECTOR 2 :
MAGNITUDE: 6.9282032303
ANGLE WITH X-AXIS: 54.73561073261
ANGLE WITH Y-AXIS: 54.73561078261
ANGLE WITH Z-AXIS: 54.73561073261

ANGLE BETWEEN VECTORS: 35.26438998282

MORE DATA (1=YES, 0=NO)? 0

END PROGRAM
```

```
10    PRINT "ANALYSIS OF TWO VECTORS"
20    PRINT
30    DIM X(2), Y(2), Z(2), M(2)
39    REM - STATEMENTS 40 TO 70 REQUEST VECTOR COORDINATES
40    PRINT "VECTOR 1: X,Y,Z";
50    INPUT X(1),Y(1),Z(1)
60    PRINT "VECTOR 2: X,Y,Z";
70    INPUT X(2),Y(2),Z(2)
80    PRINT
89    REM - LOOP TO ANALYZE BOTH VECTORS
90    FOR I=1  TO 2
99    REM - CALCULATE MAGNITUDE, PRINT
100   M(I)=SQR(X(I)↑2+Y(I)↑2+Z(I)↑2)
109   REM - IS VECTOR A POINT? IF YES, CANNOT COMPUTE AN ANGLE
110   IF M(I)=0  THEN  220
120   PRINT "VECTOR";I;":"
130   PRINT "MAGNITUDE:";M(I)
139   REM - CONVERSION FACTOR FOR RADIANS TO DEGREES
140   S=57.29578
149   REM - CALCULATE ANGLE BETWEEN VECTOR AND X-AXIS, PRINT
150   J=X(I)/M(I)
160   PRINT "ANGLE WITH X-AXIS:";ARCCOS(J)*S
169   REM - CALCULATE ANGLE BETWEEN VECTOR AND Y-AXIS, PRINT
170   J=Y(I)/M(I)
180   PRINT "ANGLE WITH Y-AXIS:";ARCCOS(J)*S
189   REM - CALCULATE ANGLE BETWEEN VECTOR AND Z-AXIS, PRINT
190   J=Z(I)/M(I)
200   PRINT "ANGLE WITH Z-AXIS:";ARCCOS(J)*S
210   PRINT
220   NEXT I
230   J=0
239   REM - IF EITHER VECTOR A POINT, CANNOT COMPUTE ANGLE
240   IF M(1)=0  THEN  310
250   IF M(2)=0  THEN  310
259   REM - CALCULATE ANGLE BETWEEN VECTORS
260   J=(X(1)*X(2)+Y(1)*Y(2)+Z(1)*Z(2))/M(1)/M(2)
269   REM - ARE THE VECTORS PERPENDICULAR?
270   IF J<>0  THEN  300
280   J=90
290   GOTO  310
299   REM - CALCULATE ANGLE IN DEGREES, PRINT
300   J=ARCCOS(J)*S
310   PRINT "ANGLE BETWEEN VECTORS:";J
320   PRINT
329   REM - RESTART OR END PROGRAM?
330   PRINT "MORE DATA (1=YES, 0=NO)";
340   INPUT Z
350   IF Z=1  THEN  20
360   END
```

Operations on Two Vectors

This program performs four operations on two vectors given in three space. The operations performed are

1) Addition
2) Subtraction
3) Scalar (dot) product
4) Cross product

Example:

Vectors are drawn from the origin to two points A(5,-1,2) and B(1,4,9). Add, subtract, and find the dot and cross product of these vectors.

```
:RUN
OPERATIONS ON TWO VECTORS

VECTOR A: X,Y,Z COORDINATES? 5,-1,2
VECTOR B: X,Y,Z COORDINATES? 1,4,9

A+B= 6 , 3 , 11
A-B= 4 ,-5 ,-7
A.B= 19
A*B=-17 ,-43 , 21

MORE DATA? (1=YES, 0=NO)? 0

END PROGRAM
```

```
PROGRAM LISTING

  10    PRINT "OPERATIONS ON TWO VECTORS"
  20    PRINT
  30    PRINT "VECTOR A: X;Y,Z COORDINATES";
  40    INPUT X1,Y1,Z1
  50    PRINT "VECTOR B: X,Y,Z COORDINATES";
  60    INPUT X2,Y2,Z2
  70    PRINT
  79    REM - PERFORM VECTOR ADDITION, PRINT RESULTING VECTOR COORDINATES
  80    PRINT "A+B=";X1+X2;",";Y1+Y2;",";Z1+Z2
  89    REM - PERFORM VECTOR SUBTRACTION, PRINT RESULTING VECTOR COORDINATES
  90    PRINT "A-B=";X1-X2;",";Y1-Y2;",";Z1-Z2
  99    REM - CALCULATE DOT PRODUCT, PRINT
 100    PRINT "A.B=";X1*X2+Y1*Y2+Z1*Z2
 109    REM - CALCULATE CROSS PRODUCT, PRINT RESULTING VECTOR COORDINATES
 110    PRINT "A*B=";Y1*Z2-Z1*Y2;",";Z1*X2-X1*Z2;",";X1*Y2-Y1*X2
 120    PRINT
 129    REM - RESTART OR END PROGRAM?
 130    PRINT "MORE DATA? (1=YES, 0=NO)";.
 140    INPUT X
 150    IF X=1  THEN    20
 160    END
```

Angle Conversion: Radians to Degrees

This program converts an angle given in radians to degrees, minutes and seconds.

Example:

How many degrees, minutes and seconds are there in an angle of 2.5 radians? In 118 radians?

```
:RUN
ANGLE CONVERSION: RADIANS TO DEGREES

ANGLE IN RADIANS (ENTER 0 TO END PROGRAM)? 2.5
    DEGREES = 143
    MINUTES = 14
    SECONDS = 22.01

ANGLE IN RADIANS? 118
    DEGREES = 280
    MINUTES = 54
    SECONDS = 6.78

ANGLE IN RADIANS? 0

END PROGRAM
```

```
PROGRAM LISTING

   10   PRINT "ANGLE CONVERSION: RADIANS TO DEGREES"
   20   PRINT
   30   PRINT "ANGLE IN RADIANS (ENTER 0 TO END PROGRAM)";
   40   GOTO   60
   50   PRINT "ANGLE IN RADIANS";
   60   INPUT R
   69   REM - TEST FOR END OF PROGRAM
   70   IF R=0   THEN   170
   79   REM - CONVERT RADIANS TO SECONDS
   80   A=3600*180*R/3.1415927
   89   REM - CALCULATE NUMBER OF WHOLE DEGREES
   90   D=INT(A/3600)
   99   REM - CALCULATE NUMBER OF FULL CIRCLES
  100   D1=INT(D/360)
  109   REM - CALCULATE DEGREES OF ANGLE WITHIN 360 DEGREES, PRINT
  110   PRINT "    DEGREES =";D-360*D1
  119   REM - CALCULATE MINUTES, PRINT
  120   PRINT "    MINUTES =";INT((A-D*3600)/60)
  129   REM - CALCULATE SECONDS, ROUND OFF, PRINT
  130   S=A-D*3600-(INT((A-D*3600)/60))*60
  140   PRINT "    SECONDS =";INT(100*S+.5)/100
  150   PRINT
  159   REM RESTART PROGRAM
  160   GOTO   50
  170   END
```

OPTION

You may prefer your answer in degrees and decimals of degrees rather than degrees, minutes and seconds. The program changes necessary are listed following the example below.

Example:

How many degrees are there in an angle of 2.5 radians?

```
:RUN
ANGLE CONVERSION: RADIANS TO DEGREES

ANGLE IN RADIANS (ENTER 0 TO END PROGRAM)? 2.5
    DEGREES = 143

ANGLE IN RADIANS? 0

END PROGRAM


PROGRAM LISTING

    1    REM - OPTION 110
   10    PRINT "ANGLE CONVERSION: RADIANS TO DEGREES"
    .
    .
    .
  109    REM - CALCULATE DEGREES OF ANGLE WITHIN 360 DEGREES, PRINT
  110    PRINT "   DEGREES =";INT((D-360*D1)*100+.5)/100
  150    PRINT
    .
    .
    .
  170    END
```

Angle Conversion: Degrees to Radians

This program converts an angle given in degrees, minutes and seconds to radians.

Examples:

An angle measures 30 degrees, 5 minutes and 3 seconds. What would be the measure of this angle in radians?

What would be the radian measurement of two angles measuring 278°, 19', 54'' and 721°, 0', 0''?

```
:RUN
ANGLE CONVERSION: DEGREES TO RADIANS

(TO END PROGRAM ENTER 0,0,0)
ANGLE IN DEGREES,MINUTES,SECONDS? 30,5,3
RADIANS = .5250676852416

ANGLE IN DEGREES,MINUTES,SECONDS? 278,19,54
RADIANS = 4.857803294516

ANGLE IN DEGREES,MINUTES,SECONDS? 721,0,0
RADIANS = 1.74514900E-02

ANGLE IN DEGREES,MINUTES,SECONDS? 0,0,0

END PROGRAM
```

```
PROGRAM LISTING

  10    PRINT "ANGLE CONVERSION: DEGREES TO RADIANS"
  20    PRINT
  30    PRINT "(TO END PROGRAM ENTER 0,0,0)"
  40    PRINT "ANGLE IN DEGREES,MINUTES,SECONDS";
  50    INPUT D,M,S
  59    REM - TEST FOR END OF PROGRAM
  60    IF D<>0  THEN  100
  70    IF M<>0  THEN  100
  80    IF S<>0  THEN  100
  90    GOTO  150
  99    REM - CONVERT DEGREES, MINUTES, SECONDS TO DEGREES
 100    A=D+M/60+S/3600
 109    REM - CALCULATE NUMBER OF COMPLETE CIRCLES
 110    R=INT(A/360)
 119    REM - CALCULATE ANGLE WITHIN 360 DEGREES, PRINT
 120    PRINT "RADIANS =";A*.01745329-R*6.2831853
 130    PRINT
 139    REM - RESTART PROGRAM
 140    GOTO   40
 150    END
```

OPTION

It may be more convenient for you to enter the angle in degrees and fractions of degrees rather than degrees, minutes and seconds. The program changes necessary are listed following the example below.

Example:

How many radians are in an angle measuring 33.08°? 90°?

```
:RUN
ANGLE CONVERSION: DEGREES TO RADIANS

(TO END PROGRAM ENTER 0)
ANGLE IN DEGREES? 33.08
RADIANS = .5773548332

ANGLE IN DEGREES? 90
RADIANS = 1.5707961

ANGLE IN DEGREES? 0

END PROGRAM


PROGRAM LISTING

    1    REM - OPTION 30-60
   10    PRINT "ANGLE CONVERSION: DEGREES TO RADIANS"
   20    PRINT
   30    PRINT "(TO END PROGRAM ENTER 0)"
   40    PRINT "ANGLE IN DEGREES";
   50    INPUT A
   59    REM - TEST FOR END OF PROGRAM
   60    IF A=0  THEN  150
  109    REM - CALCULATE NUMBER OF COMPLETE CIRCLES
    .
    .
    .
  150    END
```

Coordinate Conversion

This program converts the coordinates of a point given in Cartesian coordinates to polar coordinates, and vice versa.

The formulas for the conversions are:

$$r = \sqrt{x^2 + y^2}$$

$$A = \text{arctangent}\,(y/x)$$

$$x = r \cdot \text{cosine}\,(A)$$

$$y = r \cdot \text{sine}\,(A)$$

where: x = abscissa ⎱
  y = ordinate ⎰ Cartesian coordinates
  r = magnitude of ray ⎱
  A = angle (in degrees) ⎰ polar coordinates

Examples:

Find Cartesian coordinates of the point (2,30.5°) given in polar coordinates.

If a point is at (7,18) in the Cartesian system, what are its coordinates in the polar system?

A point is located at (0,-46.8). What is its location in polar coordinates?


```
:RUN
COORDINATE CONVERSION

                ( 1=CARTESIAN TO POLAR)
                (-1=POLAR TO CARTESIAN)
                ( 0=END PROGRAM)
WHICH DIRECTION? -1
R,A? 2,30.5
X = 1.72 ,  Y = 1.02
WHICH DIRECTION? 1
X,Y? 7,18
R = 19.31 ,  A = 68.75
WHICH DIRECTION? 1
X,Y? 0,-46.8
R = 46.8 ,  A = 270
WHICH DIRECTION? 0

END PROGRAM
```

```
 10    PRINT "COORDINATE CONVERSION"
 20    PRINT
 30    PRINT "              ( 1=CARTESIAN TO POLAR)"
 40    PRINT "              (-1=POLAR TO CARTESIAN)"
 50    PRINT "              ( 0=END PROGRAM)"
 60    PRINT "WHICH DIRECTION";
 70    INPUT D
 79    REM - END PROGRAM?
 80    IF D=0   THEN   380
 89    REM - DIRECT PROGRAM TO PERFORM PROPER CONVERSION
 90    IF D=-1  THEN   320
 98    REM - CONVERT FROM CARTESIAN COORDINATES TO POLAR COORDINATES
 99    REM - ENTER CARTESIAN COORDINATES (ABSCISSA, ORDINATE)
100    PRINT "X,Y";
110    INPUT X,Y
119    REM - POINT ON Y-AXIS?
120    IF X=0   THEN   170
129    REM - POINT ON X-AXIS?
130    IF Y=0   THEN   260
139    REM - COMPUTE POLAR COORDINATES, ROUND OFF, PRINT
140    PRINT "R =";INT(SGN(X)*SQR(X↑2+Y↑2)*100+.5)/100;",";
150    PRINT "  A =";INT(ATN(Y/X)*180/3.1415927*100+.5)/100
160    GOTO   60
169    REM - POINT IS ON Y-AXIS; AT ORIGIN?
170    IF Y=0   THEN   240
180    PRINT "R =";ABS(Y);",";
189    REM - IS POINT ABOVE OR BELOW ORIGIN?
190    IF Y<0   THEN   220
200    PRINT "  A = 90"
210    GOTO   60
220    PRINT "  A = 270"
230    GOTO   60
239    REM - POINT IS AT ORIGIN
240    PRINT "R = 0,   A = 0"
250    GOTO   60
259    REM - POINT IS ON X-AXIS
260    PRINT "R =";ABS(X);",";
269    REM - IS POINT TO LEFT OR RIGHT OF ORIGIN?
270    IF X<0   THEN   300
280    PRINT "  A = 0"
290    GOTO   60
300    PRINT "  A = 180"
310    GOTO   60
318    REM - CONVERT FROM POLAR COORDIATES TO CARTESIAN COORDINATES
319    REM - ENTER POLAR COORDINATES (MAGNITUDE OF RAY, ANGLE)
320    PRINT "R,A";
330    INPUT R,A
339    REM - CONVERT FROM DEGREES TO RADIANS
340    M=(A-INT(A/360)*360)*3.1415927/180
349    REM - CALCULATE CARTESIAN COORDINATES, ROUND OFF, PRINT
350    PRINT "X =";INT(R*COS(M)*100+.5)/100;",";
360    PRINT "  Y =";INT(R*SIN(M)*100+.5)/100
370    GOTO   60
380    END
```

Coordinate Plot

This program plots points on a set of coordinate axes. You must provide the *x* - and *y* -coordinates of all points to be plotted, the endpoints of the *x* - and *y* -axes, and the increment between points on each axis.

The graph is unconventional in that its *x* -axis runs vertically while its *y* -axis runs horizontally. In addition, the axes do not necessarily intersect at zero. A reminder as to where the axes intersect is printed at the top of each graph.

The limit on the number of points plotted may be increased or decreased by altering statement 30 in the following manner:

$$30 \; \text{DIM} \; X(N+1), Y(N+1)$$

where N = the maximum number of points you wish to plot.

The length of the *y* -axis is limited by the width of your output device. This program tests for a length not to exceed 70 spaces. The test at statement 90 should be altered to accommodate your particular output device. For an output device with a line width of 112 characters you might enter:

$$90 \; \text{IF} \; B2 <= 108 \; \text{THEN} \; 120$$

Example:

The heights of twelve men and their sons are recorded in the table below. Plot the data points.

father	65	63	67	64	68	62	70	66	68	67	69	71
son	68	66	68	65	69	66	68	65	71	67	68	70

height in inches

```
:30 DIM X(13),Y(13)
:RUN
COORDINATE PLOT

X-AXIS: LEFT ENDPOINT, RIGHT ENDPOINT, INCREMENT? 62,73,.5
Y-AXIS: LOWER ENDPOINT, UPPER ENDPOINT, INCREMENT? 62,73,.25
NUMBER OF POINTS TO BE PLOTTED? 12
COORDINATES OF POINT   1 ? 65,68
               POINT   2 ? 63,66
               POINT   3 ? 67,68
               POINT   4 ? 64,55
               POINT   5 ? 68,69
               POINT   6 ? 62,56
               POINT   7 ? 70,68
               POINT   8 ? 66,55
               POINT   9 ? 68,71
               POINT  10 ? 67,67
               POINT  11 ? 69,68
               POINT  12 ? 71,70
```

INTERSECTION OF AXES AT (62 , 62)

```
****************+****************************Y
*
*                    +
*
*                 +
*
*                      +
*
*              +
*
*                +   +
*
*                    +      +
*
*                +
*
*                +
*
*                   +
*
*
*
X
```

END PROGRAM

PROGRAM LISTING

```
    10    PRINT   "COORDINATE PLOT"
    20    PRINT
    28    REM - DIMENSION OF X() AND Y() SHOULD BE LIMITED TO (N+1);
    29    REM - WHERE N=THE NUMBER OF POINTS BEING PLOTTED, MAX. LIMIT  99
    30    DIM X(100),Y(100)
    39    REM - INPUT INFORMATION TO SET UP AXES
    40    PRINT   "X-AXIS: LEFT ENDPOINT, RIGHT ENDPOINT, INCREMENT";
    50    INPUT A1, A2, A3
    60    PRINT   "Y-AXIS: LOWER ENDPOINT, UPPER ENDPOINT, INCREMENT";
    70    INPUT B1, B2, B3
    80    B2=(B2-B1)/B3
    88    REM - Y-AXIS TOO LONG FOR OUTPUT DEVICE? IF YES, CHANGE ENDPOINTS
    89    REM - OR INCREASE INCREMENT
    90    IF B2<=70  THEN  120
   100    PRINT "Y-RANGE TOO LARGE"
   110    GOTO    60
   120    PRINT "NUMBER OF POINTS TO BE PLOTTED";
   130    INPUT N
   139    REM - NO POINTS TO PLOT? END PROGRAM
   140    IF N=0   THEN 1070
   149    REM - TOO MANY POINTS? IF YES, REENTER NUMBER OF POINTS
   150    IF N<=99   THEN   180
   160    PRINT "TOO MANY POINTS"
   170    GOTO   120
```

```
179    REM - LOOP TO INPUT X,Y COORDINATES FOR EACH POINT
180    FOR I=1   TO N
190    IF I>1   THEN   220
200    PRINT "COORDINATES OF POINT ";I;
210    GOTO   230
220    PRINT "                    POINT ";I;
230    INPUT X(I)   Y(I)
239    REM - ROUND OFF EACH X,Y TO NEAREST INCREMENT ON AXIS
240    X(I)=INT((X(I)-A1)/A3+.5)
250    Y(I)=INT((Y(I)-B1)/B3+.5)
260    NEXT I
269    REM - CALCULATE ADDITIONAL X AND Y COORDINATE
270    Y(N+1)=INT(B2+.5)+1
280    X(N+1)=INT((A2-A1)/A3+.5)+1
290    PRINT
299    REM - NOTE WHERE AXES CROSS
300    PRINT "INTERSECTION OF AXES AT (";A1;",";B1;")"
310    PRINT
319    REM - SORT COORDINATES; REORDER X(1) TO X(N) SMALLEST TO LARGEST
320    FOR J=1   TO N
330    FOR I=1   TO N-J
340    A=X(I)
350    B=Y(I)
360    C=X(I+1)
370    D=Y(I+1)
380    IF A<C   THEN   430
390    X(I)=C
400    Y(I)=D
410    X(I+1)=A
420    Y(I+1)=B
430    NEXT I
440    NEXT J
449    REM - NEXT POINT TO BE PLOTTED STORED IN T
450    T=1
459    REM - SKIP POINTS OUT OF X-POSITIVE RANGE
460    FOR P=0   TO N-1
470    IF X(P+1)>=0   THEN   490
480    NEXT P
489    REM - LOOP TO CALL UP EACH X-INCREMENT FOR LINES OF PRINT
490    FOR I=0   TO INT((A2-A1)/A3+.5)
500    T=T+P
509    REM - COUNT NUMBER OF POINTS TO BE PLOTTED ON EACH LINE IN P
510    P=0
519    REM - ALL POINTS PLOTTED?
520    IF T>N   THEN   540
529    REM - X-VALUE ON X-LINE? IF YES, TEST FOR Y
530    IF X(T)=I   THEN   590
539    REM - FIRST LINE? IF YES, Y-AXIS MUST BE PLOTTED
540    IF I=0   THEN   570
549    REM - PLOT X-AXIS
550    PRINT "*";
560    GOTO 1040
570    S=N+1
580    GOTO   920
590    FOR L=T   TO N
599    REM - NEXT POINT PLOTTED ON SAME LINE?
600    IF X(L)>X(T)   THEN   630
```

```
609    REM - COUNT POINTS TO BE PLOTTED ON EACH LINE
610    P=P+1
620    NEXT L
629    REM - PLOT ONE POINT
630    IF P=1   THEN   730
638    REM - LOOP TO SORT Y-COORDINATES WITH EQUAL X-COORDINATES;
639    REM - REORDER SMALLEST TO LARGEST
640    FOR J=1   TO P
650    FOR L=1   TO P-J
660    D=Y(T+L-1)
670    B=Y(T+L)
680    IF D<=B   THEN   710
690    Y(T+L-1)=B
700    Y(T+L)=D
710    NEXT L
720    NEXT J
730    FOR L=0   TO P-1
740    Z=Y(T+L)
749    REM - TEST FOR OUT-OF-RANGE Y-COORDINATE
750    IF Z>=0   THEN   770
760    NEXT L
769    REM - POINT TO BE PLOTTED ON X-AXIS?
770    IF I=0   THEN   910
779    REM - POINT TO BE PLOTTED ON Y-AXIS?
780    IF Z=0   THEN   800
789    REM - PLOT X-AXIS
790    PRINT "*";
800    IF L=P-1   THEN   870
810    FOR J=L   TO P-1
819    REM - TEST FOR OUT-OF-RANGE Y-COORDINATE
820    IF Z>B2   THEN 1040
829    REM - BYPASS DUPLICATE COORDINATES
830    IF Y(T+J)=Z   THEN   860
839    REM - PLOT POINT
840    PRINT TAB(Z);"+";
850    Z=Y(T+J)
860    NEXT J
869    REM - TEST FOR OUT-OF-RANGE Y-COORDINATE
870    IF Z<0   THEN 1040
880    IF Z>B2   THEN 1040
889    REM - PLOT POINT
890    PRINT TAB(Z);"+";
900    GOTO 1040
910    S=T+L
919    REM - LOOP TO ESTABLISH PRINT FOR FIRST LINE
920    FOR J=0   TO B2
929    REM - POINT TO BE PLOTTED?
930    IF Y(S)<>J   THEN 1010
939    REM - PLOT POINT
940    PRINT "+";
949    REM - BYPASS DUPLICATE COORDINATES
950    FOR K=S   TO T+P-1
960    IF Y(K)=Y(S)   THEN   990
970    S=K
980    GOTO 1020
990    NEXT K
1000   GOTO 1020
```

```
1009   REM - PLOT Y-AXIS
1010   PRINT "*";
1020   NEXT J
1029   REM - LABEL Y-AXIS
1030   PRINT "Y";
1039   REM - ADVANCE OUTPUT DEVICE TO NEXT LINE
1040   PRINT
1050   NEXT I
1059   REM - LABEL X-AXIS
1060   PRINT "X"
1070   END
```

Plot of Polar Equation

This program plots a given function in polar coordinates. There are up to 90 points plotted, one every four degrees. (Some points may overlap.)

The graph is conventional in that the x -axis runs horizontally, the y -axis runs vertically, and they intersect at zero. You need only specify the absolute value of the endpoints.

The increment between each point on the x - and y -axes is adjusted so that a value of one on either axis is equidistant from zero. This allows the function to be plotted with minimal distortion. An adjustment of each increment is necessary because of different spacing horizontally and vertically on an output device. (This program assumes ten spaces per inch horizontally and six spaces per inch vertically. If your output device differs, the graph may be distorted.)

It is necessary for you to enter the function to be plotted before you run the program. The function must be entered as a function of d. $f(d)$ will be entered and set equal to F at line 130. For example, the function $f(d) = 2 \cdot (1-\cos(d))$ will be entered as follows:

```
130 F=2*(1-COS(D))
```

(Continued on next page)

Example:

Plot the equation $f(d) = 2 \cdot (1 - \cos(d))$.

```
:130 F=2*(1-COS(D))
:RUN
PLOT OF POLAR EQUATION

ABSOLUTE VALUE OF ENDPOINTS? 4

INCREMENT OF X-AXIS = .1333333333333
INCREMENT OF Y-AXIS = .2222222222222

                                        *
                                        *
                                        *
                                        *
                                        *
                                        *
                                        *
                   +  +  +              *
               +  +  +        +  ++     *
            +  +                   ++  *
         +                        +*+
         +                        *+
        +                         *  ++
       +                          *   +
      +                           *      +
                                  *      +
    <                             *      +
                                  *      +
 +                                *   +
 +                                *  ++
+*************************************++*+*********************************X
 +                                *  ++
 +                                *   +
     <                            *      +
       +                          *      +
        +                         *      +
         +                        *   +
          +                       * ++
           +                      *+
             +                    +*+
         +  +                   ++ *
            +  +  +        +  ++    *
                +  +  +             *
                                   *
                                   *
                                   *
                                   *
                                   *
                                   *
                                   *
                                   Y

END PROGRAM
```

```
10    PRINT "PLOT OF POLAR EQUATION"
20    PRINT
28    REM - COORDINATE ARRAYS SET FOR 90 POINTS;
29    REM - ONE EXTRA X-COORDINATE IS CALCULATED IN PROGRAM
30    DIM X(91),Y(90)
39    REM - NUMBER OF POINTS TO BE CALCULATED
40    N=90
49    REM - ABSOLUTE VALUE OF ALL ENDPOINTS ARE EQUAL
50    PRINT "ABSOLUTE VALUE OF ENDPOINTS";
60    INPUT Z
70    PRINT
79    REM - CALCULATE INCREMENTS OF AXES ACCORDING TO CHARACTERS PER AX
   IS
80    PRINT "INCREMENT OF X-AXIS =";Z/30
90    PRINT "INCREMENT OF Y-AXIS =";Z/18
100   PRINT
110   FOR I=1  TO N
119   REM - CONVERT DEGREES TO RADIANS
120   D=.06981317*I
130   REM - ENTER FUNCTION HERE (F="FUNCTION")
139   REM - CALCULATE EACH CARTESIAN COORDINATE, ROUND OFF TO NEAREST I
   NCREMENT ON AXIS
140   X(I)=INT(((F*COS(D)/Z+1)*30)+.5)
150   Y(I)=INT(((-F*SIN(D)/Z+1)*18)+.5)
160   NEXT I
169   REM - SORT COORDINATES; REORDER Y(1) TO Y(N) SMALLEST TO LARGEST
170   FOR J=1  TO N
180   FOR I=1  TO N-J
190   A=X(I)
200   B=Y(I)
210   IF B<=Y(I+1)  THEN  260
220   X(I)=X(I+1)
230   Y(I)=Y(I+1)
240   X(I+1)=A
250   Y(I+1)=B
260   NEXT I
270   NEXT J
279   REM - NEXT POINT TO BE PLOTTED STORED IN T
280   T=1
289   REM - SKIP POINTS OUT OF Y-POSITIVE RANGE
290   FOR P=0  TO N-1
300   IF Y(P+1)>=0  THEN  320
310   NEXT P
319   REM - LOOP TO CALL UP EACH Y-INCREMENT FOR LINES OF PRINT
320   FOR I=0  TO 36
330   T=T+P
339   REM - NUMBER OF POINTS TO BE PLOTTED ON EACH LINE STORED IN P
340   P=0
349   REM - ALL POINTS PLOTTED?
350   IF T>N  THEN  370
359   REM - Y-VALUE ON Y-LINE?
360   IF Y(T)=I  THEN  420
369   REM - PRINT X-AXIS?
370   IF I=18  THEN  400
379   REM - PRINT Y-AXIS
```

```
380    PRINT TAB(30);"*";
390    GOTO  860
400    S=N+1
410    GOTO  740
420    FOR L=T  TO N
429    REM - NEXT POINT TO BE PLOTTED ON SAME LINE?
430    IF Y(L)>Y(T)  THEN  450
440    P=P+1
450    NEXT L
460    IF P=1  THEN  560
468    REM - LOOP TO SORT X-COORDINATES WITH EQUAL Y-COORDINATES;
469    REM - REORDER SMALLEST TO LARGEST
470    FOR J=1  TO P
480    FOR L=1  TO P-J
490    C=X(T+L-1)
500    A=X(T+L)
510    IF C<=A  THEN  540
520    X(T+L-1)=A
530    X(T+L)=C
540    NEXT L
550    NEXT J
559    REM - PRINT X-AXIS?
560    IF I=18  THEN  730
570    L=-1
580    S=0
590    FOR K=0  TO P-1
599    REM - MORE THAN ONE POINT TO BE PLOTTED AT SAME POINT ON GRAPH?
600    IF X(T+K)=L  THEN  690
610    L=X(T+K)
619    REM - PLOT POINT ON Y-AXIS?
620    IF L=30  THEN  660
629    REM - PLOT POINT TO THE LEFT OF Y-AXIS?
630    IF L<30  THEN  670
640    IF S=1  THEN  670
649    REM - PRINT Y-AXIS
650    PRINT TAB(30);"*";
660    S=1
669    REM - POINT OUTSIDE OF POSITIVE X-RANGE?
670    IF L>60  THEN  860
679    REM - PLOT POINT
680    PRINT TAB(L);"+";
690    NEXT K
700    IF S=1  THEN  860
709    REM - PRINT Y-AXIS
710    PRINT TAB(30);"*";
720    GOTO  860
730    S=T
739    REM - LOOP TO PRINT LINE OF X-AXIS
740    FOR J=0  TO 60
750    IF X(S)<>J  THEN  830
759    REM - PLOT POINT ON X-AXIS
760    PRINT "+";
770    FOR K=S  TO T+P-1
780    IF X(K)=X(S)  THEN  810
790    S=K
800    GOTO  840
810    NEXT K
```

```
820    GOTO   840
829    REM - PRINT X-AXIS
830    PRINT "*";
840    NEXT J
849    REM - LABEL X-AXIS
850    PRINT "X";
860    PRINT
870    NEXT I
879    REM - LABEL Y-AXIS
880    PRINT TAB(30);"Y"
890    END
```

Plot of Functions

This program calculates and plots up to nine functions. All functions must be functions of x, and all will be plotted on the same set of axes.

To set up the axes you must input the endpoints of the x- and y-axes. You must also state the increment by which the points on each axis are to be increased.

The graph is unconventional in that its x-axis runs vertically while its y-axis runs horizontally. To read the graph you must either turn your output 90° counterclockwise or mentally adjust to the change in convention.

The graph is also unconventional in that its axes do not necessarily cross at zero. A reminder as to where the axes cross is printed at the top of each graph.

You must enter the functions to be plotted as program statements prior to running the program. Statement numbers 221 to 229 are reserved for this purpose. Functions must be entered in the number sequence Y(1), Y(2),. . . Y(9). For example, if you wish to plot the functions $f(x) = 2x + 1$ and $f(x) = \sqrt{x}$, you must type:

```
221 Y(1)=2*X+1
222 Y(2)=SQR(X)
```

The length of the y-axis is limited by the width of your output device. This program tests for a length not to exceed 70 spaces. The test at statement 140 should be altered to accommodate your particular output device. For example, an output device with a line width of 64 characters would accommodate a graph 62 spaces wide. You would change statement 140 to:

```
140 IF Y2<=62 THEN 170
```

Example:

Plot the equations $f(x) = \cos(x)$ and $f(x) = \sin(x)$.

```
:221 Y(1)=COS(X)
:222 Y(2)=SIN(X)
:RUN
PLOT OF FUNCTIONS

NUMBER OF FUNCTIONS TO BE PLOTTED? 2
X-AXIS:LEFT ENDPOINT,RIGHT ENDPOINT,INCREMENT? -5,5,.25
Y-AXIS:LOWER ENDPOINT,UPPER ENDPOINT,INCREMENT? -2,2,.1
```

X-AXIS CROSSES Y-AXIS AT Y=-2
Y-AXIS CROSSES X-AXIS AT X=-5

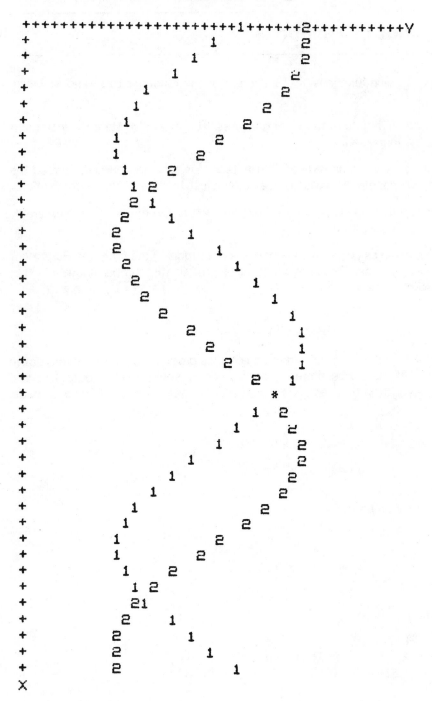

END PROGRAM

```
 10    PRINT "PLOT OF FUNCTIONS"
 20    PRINT
 29    REM - NUMBER OF FUNCTIONS WHICH CAN BE PLOTTED IS LIMITED TO 9
 30    DIM Y(9),A$(11)
 40    FOR I=1  TO 11
 49    REM - GET VALUES FOR A$-ARRAY FROM DATA TABLE AT STATEMENT 470
 50    READ A$(I)
 60    NEXT I
 69    REM - STATEMENTS 70 TO 120 REQUEST USER INPUT
 70    PRINT "NUMBER OF FUNCTIONS TO BE PLOTTED";
 80    INPUT N
 90    PRINT "X-AXIS:LEFT ENDPOINT,RIGHT ENDPOINT,INCREMENT";
100    INPUT X1,X2,X3
110    PRINT "Y-AXIS:LOWER ENDPOINT,UPPER ENDPOINT,INCREMENT";
120    INPUT Y1,Y2,Y3
129    REM - CALCULATE NUMBER OF SPACES ON Y-AXIS
130    Y2=(Y2-Y1)/Y3
138    REM - TEST FOR A Y-AXIS TOO LONG FOR OUTPUT DEVICE.  IF YES, THEN
139    REM - LESSEN RANGE OR INCREASE INCREMENT
140    IF Y2<=70  THEN  170
150    PRINT "Y-RANGE TOO LARGE"
160    GOTO  110
170    PRINT
180    PRINT
189    REM - MAKE NOTE OF WHERE AXES CROSS
190    PRINT "X-AXIS CROSSES Y-AXIS AT Y=";Y1
200    PRINT "Y-AXIS CROSSES X-AXIS AT X=";X1
210    PRINT
219    REM - SET UP LOOP TO READ VALUE AT EACH X-INCREMENT
220    FOR X=X1  TO X2  STEP X3
221    REM - FUNCTIONS Y(1) TO Y(9) SHOULD BE ENTERED AT LINES 221 TO 229
230    FOR I=1  TO N
239    REM - ESTABLISH THE ROUNDED VALUE OF Y FOR EACH X-INCREMENT VALUE
240    Y(I)=INT((Y(I)-Y1)/Y3+.5)
250    NEXT I
259    REM - LOOP TO READ VALUE OF EACH Y-INCREMENT
260    FOR I=0  TO Y2
269    REM - S COUNTS THE NUMBER OF VALUES AT EACH Y-INCREMENT FOR EACH X
270    S=0
280    FOR J=1  TO N
289    REM - PLOT A POINT ON THIS SPOT? IF YES, STORE FUNCTION NUMBER IN T
290    IF Y(J)<>I  THEN  320
300    S=S+1
310    T=J
320    NEXT J
327    REM - TEST FOR NUMBER OF POINTS TO PLOT ON EACH SPOT;
329    REM - IF 0 PRINT "+" (FIRST LINE ONLY), IF 1 PRINT FUNCTION NUMBER,
       IF 2 OR MORE PRINT "*"
330    IF S>0  THEN  360
340    PRINT A$(SGN(I)+10);
350    GOTO  400
360    IF S>1  THEN  390
370    PRINT A$ (T);
380    GOTO  400
390    PRINT "*";
```

```
400    NEXT I
409    REM - LABEL AXES AT THE LAST SPACE ON EACH AXIS
410    IF X>X1   THEN   430
420    PRINT "Y";
429    REM - ADVANCE PRINTER TO NEXT LINE
430    PRINT
439    REM - PRINT SPACE INSTEAD OF "+" AFTER FIRST LINE OF PRINT (Y-AXIS
440    A$(11)=" "
450    NEXT X
460    PRINT "X"
470    DATA "1","2","3","4","5","6","7","8","9","+","+"
480    END
```

Linear Interpolation

This program calculates the y-coordinates of points on a line given their x-coordinates. It is necessary to know coordinates of two points on the same line.

The point is interpolated using the following formula:

$$y = y_1 + \frac{(y_2 - y_1) \cdot (x - x_1)}{(x_2 - x_1)}$$

where:
x_1, y_1 = coordinates of first point on the line
x_2, y_2 = coordinates of second point on the line
x = abscissa of point to be interpolated
y = ordinate of the point on the line with x

Examples:

A conversion table lists 60°F as 15.56°C and 90°F as 32.22°C. Calculate degrees Celsius of 73°F and 85.6°F.

A new sales tax of 17.5% has been imposed on us. What will be the tax on a sofa which sells for $455.68?

```
:RUN
LINEAR INTERPOLATION

X,Y OF FIRST POINT? 60,15.56
X,Y OF SECOND POINT? 90,32.22
INTERPOLATE: X =? 73
            Y =  22.779

MORE POINTS ON THIS LINE (1=YES, 0=NO)? 1

INTERPOLATE: X =? 85.6
            Y =  29.777

MORE POINTS ON THIS LINE (1=YES, 0=NO)? 0

NEW LINE (1=YES, 0=NO)? 1

X,Y OF FIRST POINT? 0,0
X,Y OF SECOND POINT? 100,17.5
INTERPOLATE: X =? 455.68
            Y =  79.744

MORE POINTS ON THIS LINE (1=YES, 0=NO)? 0

NEW LINE (1=YES, 0=NO)? 0

END PROGRAM
```

```
 10    PRINT "LINEAR INTERPOLATION"
 20    PRINT
 29    REM - ENTER X- AND Y-COORDINATES OF TWO POINTS ON THE LINE
 30    PRINT "X,Y OF FIRST POINT";
 40    INPUT X1,Y1
 50    PRINT "X,Y OF SECOND POINT";
 60    INPUT X2,Y2
 69    REM - ENTER X-COORDINATE OF POINT TO BE INTERPOLATED
 70    PRINT "INTERPOLATE: X =";
 80    INPUT X
 89    REM - COMPUTE CORRESPONDING Y-COORDINATE
 90    Y=Y1+(Y2-Y1)/(X2-X1)*(X-X1)
 99    REM - ROUND OFF, PRINT
100    PRINT "                   Y = ";INT(Y*1000+.5)/1000
110    PRINT
120    PRINT "MORE POINTS ON THIS LINE (1=YES, 0=NO)";
130    INPUT Z
140    PRINT
150    IF Z=1   THEN    70
159    REM - INTERPOLATE ON ANOTHER LINE?
160    PRINT "NEW LINE (1=YES, 0=NO)";
170    INPUT Z
180    IF Z=1   THEN    20
190    END
```

Curvilinear Interpolation

This program computes *y* -coordinates of points on a curve given their *x* -coordinates. You must input coordinates of known points on the curve, no two having the same abscissa.

The computations are performed using the Lagrange method of interpolation.

The number of known points on the curve which may be entered in the program is limited to 50. You may increase or decrease this limit by altering statement 30 according to the following scheme:

30 DIM X(*P*), Y(*P*)

where *P* = the number of known points on a curve.

Examples:

Consider the curve $y = x^3 - 3x + 3$. You know that the points (-3,-15), (-2,1), (-1,5), (0,3), (1,1), (2,5), and (3,21) are on the curve. What is the value of *y* when *x* = -1.65 and 0.2?

Given the following points from a sine curve, what is the sine of -2.47 and the sine of 1.5?

(-5,.958)	(0,0)
(-4,.757)	(1,.841)
(-3,-.141)	(2,.909)
(-2,-.909)	(3,.141)
(-1,-.841)	(4,-.757)
	(5,-.959)

```
:30 DIM X(11), Y(11)
:RUN
CURVILINEAR INTERPOLATION

NUMBER OF KNOWN POINTS? 7
X,Y OF POINT 1 ? -3,-15
X,Y OF POINT 2 ? -2,1
X,Y OF POINT 3 ? -1,5
X,Y OF POINT 4 ? 0,3
X,Y OF POINT 5 ? 1,1
X,Y OF POINT 6 ? 2,5
X,Y OF POINT 7 ? 3,21

INTERPOLATE: X=? -1.65
             Y= 3.457874999999

MORE X ON THIS CURVE (1=YES, 0=NO)? 1

INTERPOLATE: X=? .2
             Y= 2.408000000002

MORE X ON THIS CURVE (1=YES, 0=NO)? 0
MORE X ON ANOTHER CURVE (1=YES, 0=NO)? 1

NUMBER OF KNOWN POINTS? 11
X,Y OF POINT 1 ? -5,.958
X,Y OF POINT 2 ? -4,.757
X,Y OF POINT 3 ? -3,-.141
```

```
X,Y OF POINT 4 ? -2,-.909
X,Y OF POINT 5 ? -1,-.841
X,Y OF POINT 6 ? 0,0
X,Y OF POINT 7 ? 1,.841
X,Y OF POINT 8 ? 2,.909
X,Y OF POINT 9 ? 3,.141
X,Y OF POINT 10 ? 4,-.757
X,Y OF POINT 11 ? 5,-.959


INTERPOLATE: X=? -2.47
            Y=-.6218395970637


MORE X ON THIS CURVE (1=YES, 0=NO)? 1

INTERPOLATE: X=? 1.5
            Y= .9971637992869


MORE X ON THIS CURVE (1=YES, 0=NO)? 0
MORE X ON ANOTHER CURVE (1=YES, 0=NO)? 0


END PROGRAM



PROGRAM LISTING

    10    PRINT "CURVILINEAR INTERPOLATION"
    20    PRINT
    28    REM - LIMIT X() AND Y() TO MAXIMUM NUMBER OF POINTS KNOWN ON ANY
    29    REM - CURVE TO BE ENTERED
    30    DIM X(50), Y(50)
    40    PRINT "NUMBER OF KNOWN POINTS";
    50    INPUT P
    60    FOR I=1  TO P
    69    REM - ENTER COORDINATES OF KNOWN POINTS ON CURVE
    70    PRINT "X,Y OF POINT";I;
    80    INPUT X(I),Y(I)
    90    NEXT I
   100    PRINT
   109    REM - ENTER X-COORDINATE OF POINT TO BE INTERPOLATED
   110    PRINT "INTERPOLATE: X=";
   120    INPUT A
   130    B=0
   138    REM - COMPUTE CORRESPONDING Y-COORDINATES BY LAGRANGE METHOD OF
   139    REM - INTERPOLATION
   140    FOR J=1  TO P
   150    T=1
   160    FOR I=1  TO P
   170    IF I=J  THEN  190
   180    T=T*(A-X(I))/(X(J)-X(I))
   190    NEXT I
   200    B=B+T*Y(J)
   210    NEXT J
   219    REM - PRINT RESULTS
   220    PRINT "                  Y=";B
   230    PRINT
   239    REM - INTERPOLATE  MORE POINTS ON SAME CURVE?
   240    PRINT "MORE X ON THIS CURVE (1=YES, 0=NO)";
```

```
250    INPUT C
260    IF C=1   THEN   100
269    REM - RESTART OR END PROGRAM?
270    PRINT "MORE X ON ANOTHER CURVE (1=YES, 0=NO)";
280    INPUT C
290    IF C=1   THEN   20
300    END
```

Integration: Simpson's Rule

This program approximates the definite integral of a function. The integral is computed using Simpson's rule.

The method the program takes is optional: you must supply either the function of the curve or values of the function at specified intervals. For both methods you must enter the limits of integration and the increment between points within the limits.

If the function to be integrated is known, it must be entered before running the program. The function will be defined at line 50. For example, the function $f(x) = x^3$ will be entered as follows:

```
50 DEFFNC(X)=X↑3
```

Examples:

Find the definite integral of the function $f(x) = x^3$ between 0 and 2 with increments of .2 and .1.

What is the integral of a curve between -1 and 1 if the points known are as follows:

(-1,.54)	(.25,.969)
(-.75,.73)	(.5,.878)
(-.5,.878)	(.75,.73)
(-.25,.969)	(1,.54)
(0,1)	

```
:50 DEFFNC(X)=X↑3
:RUN
INTEGRATION: SIMPSON'S RULE

SELECTION: 1=KNOWN FORMULA, 0=UNKNOWN FORMULA? 1
LOWER, UPPER LIMIT OF INTEGRATION? 0,2
INCREMENT OF X? .2
INTEGRAL IS 4

END PROGRAM


:RUN
INTEGRATION: SIMPSON'S RULE

SELECTION: 1=KNOWN FORMULA, 0=UNKNOWN FORMULA? 1
LOWER, UPPER LIMIT OF INTEGRATION? 0,2
INCREMENT OF X? .1
INTEGRAL IS 4

END PROGRAM


:RUN
INTEGRATION: SIMPSON'S RULE

SELECTION: 1=KNOWN FORMULA, 0=UNKNOWN FORMULA? 0
LOWER, UPPER LIMIT OF INTEGRATION? -1,1
INCREMENT OF X? .25
FIRST, LAST VALUE OF F(X)? .54,.54
```

86

```
VALUE OF F(X) AT INTERVAL 1 (X=-.75 )? .73
VALUE OF F(X) AT INTERVAL 2 (X=-.5 )? .878
VALUE OF F(X) AT INTERVAL 3 (X=-.25 )? .969
VALUE OF F(X) AT INTERVAL 4 (X= 0 )? 1
VALUE OF F(X) AT INTERVAL 5 (X= .25 )? .969
VALUE OF F(X) AT INTERVAL 6 (X= .5 )? .878
VALUE OF F(X) AT INTERVAL 7 (X= .75 )? .73
INTEGRAL IS 1.682


END PROGRAM


PROGRAM LISTING

  10    PRINT "INTEGRATION: SIMPSON'S RULE"
  20    PRINT
  30    PRINT "SELECTION: 1=KNOWN FORMULA, 0=UNKNOWN FORMULA";
  40    INPUT S
  49    REM - IF FUNCTION IS KNOWN ENTER AT LINE 50 (DEFFNC(X)="FUNCTION")
  50    DEFFNC(X)=X
  60    PRINT "LOWER, UPPER LIMIT OF INTEGRATION";
  70    INPUT A,B
  80    PRINT "INCREMENT OF X";
  90    INPUT X1
  98    REM - INCREMENT MUST DIVIDE INTERVAL INTO EQUAL SUBINTERVALS;
  99    REM - IF NOT, CHANGE INCREMENT
 100    IF (B-A)/X1<>INT((B-A)/X1)  THEN   80
 110    IF S=1  THEN  150
 119    REM - FORMULA NOT KNOWN; ENTER FUNCTION VALUE AT INTEGRATION LIMITS
 120    PRINT "FIRST, LAST VALUE OF F(X)";
 130    INPUT Y1,Y2
 140    GOTO  170
 149    REM - FORMULA KNOWN; CALCULATE F(X) AT INTEGRATION LIMITS
 150    Y1=FNC(A)
 160    Y2=FNC(B)
 170    C=0
 180    D=0
 189    REM - LOOP FOR EACH SUBINTERVAL
 190    FOR I=1  TO (B-A)/X1-.5
 200    IF S=1  THEN  240
 209    REM - ENTER KNOWN FUNCTION VALUE AT EACH INTERVAL
 210    PRINT "VALUE OF F(X) AT INTERVAL";I;"(X=";A+I*X1;")";
 220    INPUT Y
 230    GOTO  250
 239    REM - CALCULATE F(X) AT EACH SUBINTERVAL
 240    Y=FNC(A+I*X1)
 249    REM - INTERVAL EVEN OR ODD?
 250    IF I/2=INT(I/2)  THEN  280
 259    REM - SUM ALL ODD-INTERVAL FUNCTION VALUES
 260    C=C+Y
 270    GOTO  290
 279    REM - SUM ALL EVEN-INTERVAL FUNCTION VALUES
 280    D=D+Y
 290    NEXT I
 299    REM - COMPUTE INTEGRAL, PRINT
 300    PRINT "INTEGRAL IS";X1/3*(Y1+4*C+2*D+Y2)
 310    END
```

Integration: Trapezoidal Rule

This program approximates the definite integral of a function. The integral is computed using the trapezoidal rule. You must provide the limits of integration and the number of intervals within the limits.

The function to be integrated must be entered before running the program. The function of x will be defined at line 30. For example, the function $f(x) = x^3$ will be entered as follows:

$$30 \text{ DEFFNC(X)=X} \uparrow 3$$

Examples:

Find the definite integral of the function $f(x) = x^3$ between 0 and 2 with 10 and 20 intervals.

Find the definite integral of the function $f(x) = x^{-2}$ between 1 and 2 and 2 and 3 using 10 subintervals.

```
:30 DEFFNC(X)=X↑3
:RUN
INTEGRATION: TRAPEZOIDAL RULE

(ENTER 0,0 TO END PROGRAM)
INTEGRATION LIMITS (LOWER, UPPER)? 0,2
NUMBER OF INTERVALS? 10
INTEGRAL = 4.04

INTEGRATION LIMITS (LOWER, UPPER)? 0,2
NUMBER OF INTERVALS? 20
INTEGRAL = 4.01

INTEGRATION LIMITS (LOWER, UPPER)? 0,0

END PROGRAM


:30 DEFFNC(X)=1/X↑2
:RUN
INTEGRATION: TRAPEZOIDAL RULE

(ENTER 0,0 TO END PROGRAM)
INTEGRATION LIMITS (LOWER, UPPER)? 1,2
NUMBER OF INTERVALS? 10
INTEGRAL = .5014551274644

INTEGRATION LIMITS (LOWER, UPPER)? 2,3
NUMBER OF INTERVALS? 10
INTEGRAL = .16681318133

INTEGRATION LIMITS (LOWER, UPPER)? 0,0

END PROGRAM
```

```
10    PRINT "INTEGRATION: TRAPEZOIDAL RULE"
20    PRINT
30    REM - ENTER FUNCTION HERE  (DEFFNC(X)="FUNCTION")
40    PRINT "(ENTER 0,0 TO END PROGRAM)"
50    PRINT "INTEGRATION LIMITS (LOWER, UPPER)";
60    INPUT A,B
69    REM - END PROGRAM?
70    IF A=B  THEN  190
80    PRINT "NUMBER OF INTERVALS";
90    INPUT N
100   I=0
109   REM - D IS THE SIZE OF EACH INTERVAL
110   D=(B-A)/N
119   REM - ADD UP THE AREA OF EACH TRAPEZOID
120   FOR J=A   TO B   STEP D
130   I=I+FNC(J)
140   NEXT J
149   REM - COMPUTE INTEGRAL, PRINT
150   I=(I-(FNC(A)+FNC(B))/2)*D
160   PRINT "INTEGRAL =";I
170   PRINT
180   GOTO   50
190   END
```

Integration: Gaussian Quadrature

This program approximates the definite integral of a function. You must provide the limits of integration and the number of intervals within the limits.

The interval of integration is divided into equal subintervals. The definite integral is computed over each subinterval using Gauss' formula. The integrals of the subintervals are summed to give the definite integral of the full interval.

You must enter the function to be integrated before running the program. The function of x will be defined at line 30. For example, the function $f(x) = x^3$ will be entered as follows:

$$30 \quad DEFFNC(X)=X\uparrow 3$$

Examples:

Find the definite integral of the function $f(x) = x^3$ between 0 and 2 with 10 and 20 subintervals.

Find the definite integral of the function $f(x) = x^{-2}$ between 1 and 2 and 3 using 10 subintervals.

```
:30 DEFFNC(X)=X↑3
:RUN
INTEGRATION: GAUSSIAN QUADRATURE

INTEGRATION LIMITS (LOWER,UPPER)? 0,2
NUMBER OF INTERVALS? 10
INTEGRAL = 4.000000027887

CHANGE DATA AND RECOMPUTE?
(0=NO, 1=NEW INTEGRATION LIMITS, 2=NEW NO. OF INTERVALS)? 2
NUMBER OF INTERVALS? 20
INTEGRAL = 4.000000027968

CHANGE DATA AND RECOMPUTE?
(0=NO, 1=NEW INTEGRATION LIMITS, 2=NEW NO. OF INTERVALS)? 0

END PROGRAM


:30 DEFFNC(X)=1/X↑2
:RUN
INTEGRATION: GAUSSIAN QUADRATURE

INTEGRATION LIMITS (LOWER,UPPER)? 1,2
NUMBER OF INTERVALS? 10
INTEGRAL = .5000000034951

CHANGE DATA AND RECOMPUTE?
(0=NO, 1=NEW INTEGRATION LIMITS, 2=NEW NO. OF INTERVALS)? 1
INTEGRATION LIMITS (LOWER,UPPER)? 2,3
NUMBER OF INTERVALS? 10
INTEGRAL = .1666666678324
```

CHANGE DATA AND RECOMPUTE?
(0=NO, 1=NEW INTEGRATION LIMITS, 2=NEW NO. OF INTERVALS)? 0

END PROGRAM

PROGRAM LISTING

```
  10   PRINT "INTEGRATION: GAUSSIAN QUADRATURE"
  20   PRINT
  30   REM - ENTER FUNCTION HERE (DEFFNC(X)="FUNCTION")
  39   REM - ABSCISSAS AND WEIGHT FACTORS FOR 20-POINT GUASSIAN INTEGRAT
    ION
  40   DATA .076526521,.15275339,.22778585,.14917299,.37370609
  50   DATA .14209611,.510867,.13168864,.63605368,.11819453
  60   DATA .74633191,.10193012,.83911697,.083276742,.91223443
  70   DATA .062672048,.96397193,.04060143,.9931286,.017614007
  80   PRINT "INTEGRATION LIMITS (LOWER,UPPER)";
  90   INPUT X,Y
 100   PRINT "NUMBER OF INTERVALS";
 110   INPUT N
 120   S=(Y-X)/N/2
 130   T=X+S
 140   R=0
 149   REM - COMPUTE INTEGRAL FOR EACH SUBINTERVAL
 150   FOR I=1  TO N
 160   P=0
 169   REM - COMPUTE SUMMATION FACTOR FOR EACH SUBINTERVAL
 170   FOR J=1  TO 10
 180   READ A,B
 190   P=P+B*(FNC(S*A+T)+FNC(T-S*A))
 200   NEXT J
 210   RESTORE
 220   R=R+P*S
 230   T=T+2*S
 240   NEXT I
 250   PRINT "INTEGRAL =";R
 260   PRINT
 270   PRINT "CHANGE DATA AND RECOMPUTE?"
 280   PRINT "(0=NO, 1=NEW INTEGRATION LIMITS, 2=NEW NO. OF INTERVALS)";
 290   INPUT S
 300   IF S=1  THEN   80
 310   IF S=2  THEN  100
 320   END
```

Derivative

This program calculates the derivative of a given function at a given point.

You must enter the function being evaluated before you run the program. The function will be entered in a definition statement at line 30. For example, to evaluate the equation $f(x) = x^2 + \cos(x)$ you would enter the following:

```
30 DEFFNC(X)=X↑2+COS(X)
```

Example:

Calculate the derivative of the equation $x^2 + \cos(x) = 0$ when $x = -1$, $x = 0$, and $x = 1$.

```
:30 DEFFNC(X)=X↑2+COS(X)
:RUN
DERIVATIVE

(ENTER X=99999 TO END PROGRAM)
DERIVATIVE AT X=? -1
                 IS-1.158528756224
DERIVATIVE AT X=? 0
                 IS 1.53600000E-09
DERIVATIVE AT X=? 1
                 IS 1.158528797696
DERIVATIVE AT X=? 99999

END PROGRAM
```

```
PROGRAM LISTING

  10    PRINT "DERIVATIVE"
  20    PRINT
  30    REM - ENTER DEFFNC(X) HERE
  40    PRINT "(ENTER X=99999 TO END PROGRAM)"
  50    PRINT "DERIVATIVE AT X=";
  60    INPUT X1
  69    REM - TEST FOR END OF PROGRAM
  70    IF X1=99999  THEN  160
  80    D=0
  89    REM - CALCULATE DIFFERENCE QUOTIENTS FOR POINTS APPROACHING X
  90    FOR N=1  TO 10
 100    D1=D
 110    X=X1+.5↑N
 120    D=(FNC(X)-FNC(X1))/(X-X1)
 130    NEXT N
 139    REM - APPROXIMATE DERIVATIVE OF FUNCTION AT X, PRINT
 140    PRINT "                   IS";2*D-D1
 149    REM - RESTART PROGRAM
 150    GOTO   50
 160    END
```

Roots of Quadratic Equations

This program calculates the roots of a quadratic equation. The equation must be in the following form:

$$ax^2 + bx + c = 0$$

where a,b,c are real coefficients.

The formula used to calculate the roots is:

$$\text{root} = \frac{-b \pm \sqrt{b^2 - 4 \cdot a \cdot c}}{2 \cdot a}$$

Example:

Compute the roots of the following equations:

$$2x^2 + x - 1 = 0$$
$$x^2 + 4x + 6 = 0$$

```
:RUN
ROOTS OF QUADRATIC EQUATIONS

COEFFICIENTS A,B,C? 2,1,-1
ROOTS (REAL):  -1 ,   .5

MORE DATA (1=YES, 0=NO)? 1

COEFFICIENTS A,B,C? 1,4,6
ROOTS (COMPLEX):  -2  + OR - 1.41421356235  I

MORE DATA (1=YES, 0=NO)? 0

END PROGRAM
```

```
PROGRAM LISTING

  10   PRINT "ROOTS OF QUADRATIC EQUATIONS"
  20   PRINT
  29   REM - ENTER COEFFICIENTS A,B,C OF A*X↑2 + B*X + C
  30   PRINT "COEFFICIENTS A,B,C";
  40   INPUT A,B,C
  50   S=B↑2-4*A*C
  60   R=SQR(ABS(S))
  69   REM - COMPLEX ROOTS?
  70   IF S<0  THEN  100
  79   REM - CALCULATE ROOTS, LABEL, PRINT
  80   PRINT "ROOTS (REAL):  ";(-B-R)/(2*A);",  ";(-B+R)/(2*A)
  90   GOTO  110
 100   PRINT "ROOTS (COMPLEX):  ";-B/(2*A);" + OR -";R/(2*A);" I"
 110   PRINT
 119   REM - RESTART OR END PROGRAM?
```

```
120    PRINT "MORE DATA (1=YES, 0=NO)";
130    INPUT X
140    IF X=1   THEN    20
150    END
```

Real Roots of Polynomials: Newton

This program calculates real roots of a polynomial with real coefficients. You must give an estimate of each root.

The calculations are performed using Newton's method for approximating roots of equations. The value of the error and derivative are included for each root calculated.

The equation you enter is presently limited to a degree of 10. You may enter a larger degree of equation by altering statements 30 and 40 of the program according to the following scheme:

$$30 \text{ DIM A}(N+1), B(N+1)$$
$$40 \text{ FOR I=1 TO } N+1$$

where N = degree of equation.

Example:

Find the roots of $4x^4 - 2.5x^2 - x + 0.5$

```
:RUN
REAL ROOTS OF POLYNOMIALS: NEWTON

DEGREE OF EQUATION? 4
COEFFICIENT A( 0 )? .5
COEFFICIENT A( 1 )? -1
COEFFICIENT A( 2 )? -2.5
COEFFICIENT A( 3 )? 0
COEFFICIENT A( 4 )? 4

GUESS? -.8

 ROOT            ERROR            DERIVATIVE
 .3035763402058 -1.40000000E-13 -2.070247000453

ANOTHER VALUE (1=YES, 0=NO)? 0
ANOTHER FUNCTION (1=YES, 0=NO)? 0

END PROGRAM
```

```
PROGRAM LISTING

  10   PRINT "REAL ROOTS OF POLYNOMIALS: NEWTON"
  20   PRINT
  28   REM - LIMIT A() AND B() TO N+1; WHEN THIS IS DONE, LOOP AT LINE 40
  29   REM - SHOULD BE SET TO TEST FROM 1 TO N+1
  30   DIM A(11),B(11)
  39   REM - INITIALIZE ARRAY VARIABLES
  40   FOR I=1  TO 11
  50   A(I)=0
  60   B(I)=0
  70   NEXT I
  80   PRINT "DEGREE OF EQUATION";
  90   INPUT N
 100   FOR I=1  TO N+1
 109   REM - ENTER COEFFICIENTS IN ORDER OF LESSER TO HIGHER DEGREE
```

```
110    PRINT "COEFFICIENT A(";I-1;")";
120    INPUT A(I)
130    NEXT I
140    FOR I=1  TO 10
149    REM - CALCULATE COEFFICIENT OF DERIVATIVE OF POLYNOMIAL
150    B(I)=A(I+1)*I
160    NEXT I
170    PRINT
179    REM - INITIALIZE GUESS
180    PRINT "GUESS";
190    INPUT X
200    Q=0
210    S=1
220    F1=0
230    F0=0
239    REM - COUNT ITERATIONS
240    Q=Q+1
250    FOR I=1  TO N+1
259    REM - CALCULATE VALUE OF FUNCTION
260    F0=F0+A(I)*S
269    REM - CALCULATE VALUE OF DERIVATIVE
270    F1=F1+B(I)*S
280    S=S*X
290    NEXT I
299    REM - TEST FOR A ZERO DERIVATIVE; IF YES, STOP SEARCH, PRINT
300    IF F1=0  THEN  360
309    REM - GET NEW GUESS USING PREVIOUS GUESS
310    S=X-F0/F1
319    REM - IF NEW GUESS = LAST GUESS THEN STOP SEARCH, PRINT
320    IF X=S  THEN  380
329    REM - SAVE LAST GUESS
330    X=S
340    IF Q>100  THEN  490
350    GOTO  210
360    PRINT "DERIVATIVE = 0 AT X =";X
370    GOTO  180
380    PRINT
390    PRINT " ROOT"," ERROR"," DERIVATIVE"
400    PRINT X,F0,F1
410    PRINT
419    REM - RERUN TO FIND ANOTHER ROOT IN SAME FUNCTION?
420    PRINT "ANOTHER VALUE (1=YES, 0=NO)";
430    INPUT A
440    IF A=1  THEN  170
449    REM - RESTART OR END PROGRAM?
450    PRINT "ANOTHER FUNCTION (1=YES, 0=NO)";
460    INPUT A
470    IF A=1  THEN  30
480    GOTO  550
489    REM - PRINT CALCULATED VALUES AFTER 100 ITERATIONS; SEARCH 100 MORE?
490    PRINT "100 ITERATIONS COMPLETED:"
500    PRINT "  X =";X;" F(X) =";F0
510    PRINT "   CONTINUE (1=YES, 0=NO)";
520    INPUT A
530    IF A=1  THEN  200
540    GOTO  420
550    END
```

Roots of Polynomials: Half-interval Search

This program calculates roots of polynomials within a given interval. The program first conducts a random search within the given interval for two points with opposite signs. If a change of sign is found, then the root is calculated by the half-interval search method. If there is no change of sign found, another interval will be asked for.

Errors may result in this program for a couple of reasons. First, a root may be calculated when it should not be. This may happen if the lowest point is so close to zero that a root is found due to round-off error. Second, two roots may be so close together that the program never finds the opposite signs between them. The result in this case is that neither root is calculated.

It is necessary to enter the equation before you run the program. The equation will be defined as a function of x at statement 30. For example, if you want to find roots of the function $f(x) = 4x^4-2.5x^2-x+.5$, you will enter:

```
30 DEFFNR(X)=4*X↑4-2.5*X↑2-X+.5
```

Example:
Find a root of the function $f(x) = 4x^4-2.5x^2- x +.5$.

```
:30 DEFFNR(X)=4*X↑4-2.5*X↑2-X+.5
:RUN
ROOTS OF POLYNOMIALS: HALF-INTERVAL SEARCH

(TO END SEARCH ENTER 0,0)
INTERVAL (LOWER, UPPER LIMIT)? -1,0
NO CHANGE OF SIGN FOUND
INTERVAL (LOWER, UPPER LIMIT)? 0,1
ROOT = .3035792010268

INTERVAL (LOWER, UPPER LIMIT)? 0,0

END PROGRAM
```

PROGRAM LISTING

```
  10   PRINT "ROOTS OF POLYNOMIALS: HALF-INTERVAL SEARCH"
  20   PRINT
  30   REM - ENTER FUNCTION (DEFFNR(X)="FUNCTION") HERE
  40   DIM D(3)
  50   PRINT "(TO END SEARCH ENTER 0,0)"
  59   REM - ESTABLISH INTERVAL OF RANDOM SEARCH
  60   PRINT "INTERVAL (LOWER, UPPER LIMIT)";
  70   INPUT A,B
  79   REM - TEST FOR USABLE LIMITS ENTERED
  80   IF A<>B  THEN  120
  89   REM - END PROGRAM?
  90   IF A=0  THEN  430
 100   PRINT "--INTERVAL LIMITS CANNOT BE EQUAL--"
```

```
110   GOTO    60
120   IF A<B  THEN  150
130   PRINT "--LOWER LIMIT MUST BE ENTERED FIRST--"
140   GOTO    60
150   A1=SGN(FNR(A))
160   B1=SGN(FNR(B))
169   REM - TEST FOR ROOT AT EITHER LIMIT
170   IF A1*B1=0   THEN   360
179   REM - TEST FOR OPPOSITE SIGNS AT INTERVAL LIMITS
180   IF A1*B1<0   THEN   280
189   REM - LOOP TO SEARCH 1000 NUMBERS FOR OPPOSITE SIGNS IN FUNCTION
190   FOR I=1  TO 1000
200   X=A+RND(2)*(B-A)
210   X1=SGN(FNR(X))
219   REM - TEST FOR ROOT AT RANDOM NUMBER; IF YES, END SEARCH, PRINT
220   IF X1=0  THEN   400
229   REM - TEST FOR OPPOSITE SIGNS AT RANDOM NUMBER AND LOWER LIMIT
230   IF A1*X1<0   THEN   270
239   REM - TRY ANOTHER RANDOM NUMBER
240   NEXT I
250   PRINT "NO CHANGE OF SIGN FOUND"
260   GOTO    60
269   REM - CHANGE OF SIGN FOUND; CALCULATE ROOT.
270   B=X
278   REM - STORE POSITIVE POINT IN D(3), NEGATIVE POINT IN D(1)
279   REM - D(1) AND D(3) BECOME INTERVAL LIMITS
280   D(2+A1)=A
290   D(2-A1)=B
299   REM - CALCULATE MIDPOINT BETWEEN THE TWO LIMITS
300   Y=(D(1)+D(3))/2
310   Y1=SGN(FNR(Y))
319   REM - TEST FOR ROOT AT MIDPOINT
320   IF Y1=0   THEN   400
329   REM - GET A NEW LIMIT TO CLOSE IN ON ROOT
330   D(2+Y1)=Y
339   REM - TEST FOR A VALUE CLOSE ENOUGH TO ZERO TO ASSUME A ROOT
340   IF ABS(D(1)-D(3))/ABS(D(1)+ABS(D(3)))<5E-6   THEN   400
349   REM - RETEST WITH NEW LIMITS
350   GOTO  300
359   REM - ROOT AT AN INTERVAL LIMIT; FIND WHICH LIMIT, PRINT
360   IF A1=0  THEN   390
370   Y=B
380   GOTO    400
390   Y=A
400   PRINT "ROOT =";Y
410   PRINT
419   REM - RESTART PROGRAM
420   GOTO    60
430   END
```

Trig Polynomial

This program solves a trigonometric function for a given angle. The function must be in the following form:

$$f(x) = A_1 \sin(x) + B_1 \cos(x) + A_2 \sin(2x) + B_2 \sin(2x) \ldots + A_n \sin(n \cdot x) + B_n \cos(n \cdot x)$$

where n = the number of pairs of coefficients.

The coefficients of the function are to be entered in a data statement at line 30. The data statement will include the number of pairs of coefficients (n) and the coefficients of the polynomial. It will be entered as follows:

$$30 \ \text{DATA} \ n, A_1, B_1, A_2, B_2, \ldots A_n, B_n$$

Example:

Solve the following equation when the angle equals 45º, 90º and 105º:

$$f(x) = \sin(x) + 2 \cdot \cos(x) - 2 \cdot \sin(2x) + \cos(2x) + 5 \cdot \sin(3x) - 3 \cdot \cos(3x)$$

```
:30 DATA 3,1,2,-2,1,5,-3
:RUN
TRIG POLYNOMIAL

(ENTER ANGLE=99999 TO END PROGRAM)
ANGLE? 45
F( 45 )= 3.095587494888

ANGLE? 90
F( 90 )=-2.831680950826

ANGLE? 105
F( 105 )=-1.546848370549

ANGLE? 99999

END PROGRAM
```

PROGRAM LISTING

```
10    PRINT "TRIG POLYNOMIAL"
20    PRINT
30    REM - ENTER NUMBER OF PAIRS OF TERMS AND COEFFICIENTS HERE
40    PRINT "(ENTER ANGLE=99999 TO END PROGRAM)"
50    PRINT "ANGLE";
60    INPUT R
69    REM - END PROGRAM?
70    IF R=99999  THEN  180
79    REM - GET NUMBER OF PAIRS OF TERMS IN POLYNOMIAL
80    READ N
89    REM - LOOP TO GET VALUES OF COEFFICIENTS FROM DATA TABLE
90    FOR I=1  TO N
100   READ A,B
```

```
109    REM - CALCULATE VALUE OF FUNCTION AT ANGLE X
110    Z=Z+A*SIN(I*R)+B*COS(I*R)
120    NEXT I
129    REM - PRINT RESULTS
130    PRINT "F(";R;")=";Z
139    REM - PREPARE TO REREAD FUNCTION COEFFICIENTS
140    RESTORE
150    PRINT
160    Z=0
169    REM - RESTART PROGRAM
170    GOTO   50
180    END
```

Simultaneous Equations

This program solves a system of linear equations. The number of unknown coefficients in each equation must equal the number of equations being solved. You must enter the coefficients of each equation.

The dimension statement at line 30 limits the number of equations which may be solved. You may change this limit according to the following scheme:

$$30 \ \text{DIM} \ A(R, R+1)$$

where $R =$ the maximum number of equations.

Example:

Solve the following system of equations:

$$x + 2x + 3x = 4$$
$$3x + 6x \qquad = 1$$
$$-3x + 4x - 2x = 0$$

```
:30 DIM A(3,4)
:RUN
SIMULTANEOUS EQUATIONS

NUMBER OF EQUATIONS? 3
COEFFICIENT MATRIX:
EQUATION 1
   COEFFICIENT 1 ? 1
   COEFFICIENT 2 ? 2
   COEFFICIENT 3 ? 3
   CONSTANT? 4
EQUATION 2
   COEFFICIENT 1 ? 3
   COEFFICIENT 2 ? 6
   COEFFICIENT 3 ? 0
   CONSTANT? 1
EQUATION 3
   COEFFICIENT 1 ? -3
   COEFFICIENT 2 ? 4
   COEFFICIENT 3 ? -2
   CONSTANT? 0

X 1 =-.356
X 2 = .344
X 3 = 1.222

END PROGRAM
```

```
10    PRINT "SIMULTANEOUS EQUATIONS"
20    PRINT
29    REM - LIMIT A() TO A(R,R+1)  WHERE R=MAX. NO. OF EQUATIONS
30    DIM A(9,10)
40    PRINT "NUMBER OF EQUATIONS";
50    INPUT R
60    PRINT "COEFFICIENT MATRIX:"
70    FOR J=1  TO R
80    PRINT "EQUATION";J
90    FOR I=1  TO R+1
100   IF I=R+1   THEN   130
110   PRINT "  COEFFICIENT";I;
120   GOTO  140
130   PRINT "  CONSTANT";
140   INPUT A(J,I)
150   NEXT I
160   NEXT J
170   FOR J=1  TO R
178   REM - STATEMENTS 180 TO 220 FIND THE FIRST EQUATION WITH A
179   REM - NON-ZERO COEFFICIENT FOR THE CURRENT COLUMN
180   FOR I=J  TO R
190   IF A(I,J)<>0  THEN   230
200   NEXT I
210   PRINT "NO UNIQUE SOLUTION"
220   GOTO  440
229   REM - STATEMENTS 230 TO 270 MOVE THAT EQUATION UP TO THE CURRENT RO
230   FOR K=1  TO R+1
240   X=A(J,K)
250   A(J,K)=A(I,K)
260   A(I,K)=X
270   NEXT K
279   REM - STATEMENTS 280 TO 310 GET A 1 COEFFICIENT IN THE FIRST NON-ZE
   O COLUMN OF THE CURRENT ROW
280   Y=1/A(J,J)
290   FOR K=1  TO R+1
300   A(J,K)=Y*A(J,K)
310   NEXT K
318   REM - STATEMENTS 320 TO 380 SUBTRACT THE CURRENT EQUATION FROM
319   REM - THE OTHER ROWS
320   FOR I=1  TO R
330   IF I=J   THEN   380
340   Y=-A(I,J)
350   FOR K=1  TO R+1
360   A(I,K)=A(I,K)+Y*A(J,K)
370   NEXT K
380   NEXT I
389   REM - THIS PROCESS IS REPEATED FOR ALL EQUATIONS
390   NEXT J
400   PRINT
409   REM - PRINT SOLUTIONS
410   FOR I=1  TO R
420   PRINT "X";I;"=";INT(A(I,R+1)*1000+.5)/1000
430   NEXT I
440   END
```

Linear Programming

Courtesy: Harold Hanes
Earlham College
Richmond, Indiana

This program uses the simplex method to solve a linear programming problem. You must provide the coefficients of the objective function and the coefficients, relation and constant of each constraint. This information is entered in DATA statements before you run the program.

After you load the program, enter the DATA statements according to the following instructions. If you run more than one problem, remember to clear out all DATA statements from the previous problem before running the new problem. Our DATA statements begin at line 3000.

1) Arrange your problem constraints according to their relation, so that the "less than" inequalities precede the equalities, which in turn precede the "greater than" inequalities.

2) Type in as DATA the coefficients of the constraints, in the order the constraints were arranged in step 1. Do not include coefficients for slack, surplus, or artificial variables. Do include a '0' coefficient for any variable that doesn't appear in a particular constraint.

3) Type in as DATA the constants of the constraints (right-hand sides of the constraints) in the same order as you entered the rows of coefficients. These values cannot be negative.

4) Type in as DATA the coefficients of the objective function.

You must select whether the problem solution is to be a minimum or maximum value. The program also asks you to enter the total number of constraints and the number of variables to allow for each, and the number of "less than", "equal" and "greater than" constraints you are considering.

The dimension statement at line 20 limits the number of variables and constraints you may enter. You can change these limits according to the following scheme:

$$20 \text{ DIM } A(C+2, V+C+G+1), B(C+2)$$

where: C = number of constraints
V = number of variables
G = number of "greater than" constraints

Example:

A manufacturer wishes to produce 100 pounds of an alloy which is 83% lead, 14% iron, and 3% antimony. He has available five alloys with the following compositions and prices:

	alloy 1	alloy 2	alloy 3	alloy 4	alloy 5
	90	80	95	70	30
	5	5	2	30	70
	5	15	3	0	0
	$6.13	$7.12	$5.85	$4.57	$3.96

How should he combine these alloys to get the desired product at minimum cost?

Note that this problem results in the following system of equations:

$$x_1 + x_2 + x_3 + x_4 + x_5 = 100$$
$$.90x_1 + .80x_2 + .95x_3 + .70x_4 + .30x_5 = 83$$
$$.05x_1 + .05x_2 + .02x_3 + .30x_4 + .70x_5 = 14$$
$$.05x_1 + .15x_2 + .03x_3 + + = 3$$
$$6.13x_1 + 7.12x_2 + 5\ 85x_3 + 4.57x_4 + 3.96x_5 = Z \text{ (min)}$$

LINEAR PROGRAMMING

TYPE '1' FOR MAXIMIZATION, OR '-1' FOR MINIMIZATION? -1
TYPE NUMBER OF CONSTRAINTS; NUMBER OF VARIABLES? 4,5
NUMBER OF LESS THAN, EQUAL, GREATER CONSTRAINTS? 0,4,0

YOUR VARIABLES 1 THROUGH 5
ARTIFICIAL VARIABLES 6 THROUGH 9

ANSWERS:
PRIMAL VARIABLES:

VARIABLES	VALUE
2	10.4347826087
3	47.82608695654
4	41.73913043478

DUAL VARIABLES:

VARIABLE	VALUE

VALUE OF OBJECTIVE FUNCTION 544.8260869565

END PROGRAM

PROGRAM LISTING

```
   10   PRINT "LINEAR PROGRAMMING"
   15   PRINT
   19   REM - LINEAR PROGRAMMING, SIMPLEX METHOD
   20   DIM A(6,10),B(6)
   30   PRINT
   40   PRINT "TYPE '1' FOR MAXIMIZATION, OR '-1' FOR MINIMIZATION";
   50   INPUT Z
   60   Z=-Z
   70   PRINT "TYPE NUMBER OF CONSTRAINTS, NUMBER OF VARIABLES";
   80   INPUT M,N
   90   PRINT "NUMBER OF LESS THAN, EQUAL, GREATER CONSTRAINTS";
  100   INPUT L,E,G
  110   IF M=L+E+G  THEN  140
  120   PRINT "DATA ON CONSTRAINTS INCONSISTENT. TRY AGAIN."
  130   GOTO   90
  139   REM - THIS IS THE INITIALIZATION ROUTINE
  140   C=N+M+G
  150   C1=C+1
  160   C2=N+L+G
  170   M1=M+1
  180   M2=M+2
  190   PRINT
  200   FOR I=1  TO M2
  210   FOR J=1  TO C1
  220   A(I,J)=0
  230   NEXT J
```

```
240    NEXT I
250    FOR I=1   TO M
260    B(I)=0
270    NEXT I
280    FOR I=1   TO M
290    FOR J=1   TO N
300    READ A(I,J)
310    IF I<=L   THEN   330
320    A(M1,J)=A(M1,J)-A(I,J)
330    NEXT J
340    IF I>L   THEN   380
350    B(I)=N+I
360    A(I,N+I)=1
370    GOTO   440
380    B(I)=N+G+I
390    A(I,N+G+I)=1
400    IF I>L+E   THEN   420
410    GOTO   440
420    A(I,N+I-E)=-1
430    A(M1,N+I-E)=1
440    NEXT I
450    FOR I=1   TO M
460    READ A(I,C1)
470    NEXT I
480    FOR J=1   TO N
490    READ A(M2,J)
500    A(M2,J)=Z*A(M2,J)
510    NEXT J
520    PRINT
540    PRINT "YOUR VARIABLES 1 THROUGH";N
550    IF L=0   THEN   570
560    PRINT "SLACK VARIABLES";N+1;"THROUGH";N+L
570    IF G=0   THEN   590
580    PRINT "SURPLUS VARIABLES";N+L+1;"THROUGH";C
590    IF L=M   THEN   780
600    PRINT "ARTIFICIAL VARIABLES";C2+1;"THROUGH";C
610    M3=M1
620    GOSUB 1040
630    PRINT
640    FOR I1=1   TO M
650    IF B(I1)<=C2   THEN   760
660    IF A(I1,C1)<=.00001   THEN   690
670    PRINT "THE PROBLEM HAS NO FEASIBLE SOLUTION."
680    GOTO 3060
690    FOR J1=1   TO C2
700    IF ABS(A(I1,J1))<=.00001   THEN   750
710    R=I1
720    S=J1
730    GOSUB 1260
740    J1=C2
750    NEXT J1
760    NEXT I1
780    PRINT
790    M3=M2
800    GOSUB 1040
```

```
830    PRINT
840    PRINT "ANSWERS:"
850    PRINT "PRIMAL VARIABLES:"
860    PRINT "VARIABLES","VALUE"
870    FOR J=1  TO C2
880    FOR I=1  TO M
890    IF B(I)<>J  THEN  920
900    PRINT J,A(I,C1)
910    I=M
920    NEXT I
930    NEXT J
940    PRINT "DUAL VARIABLES:"
950    PRINT "VARIABLE","VALUE"
960    IF L=0  THEN 1000
970    FOR I=1  TO L
980    PRINT I,-Z*A(M2,N+I)
990    NEXT I
1000   PRINT "VALUE OF OBJECTIVE FUNCTION";-Z*A(M2,C1)
1010   PRINT
1020   PRINT
1030   GOTO 3060
1038   REM - OPTIMIZATION ROUTINE
1039   REM - FIRST PRICE OUT COLUMNS
1040   P=-.00001
1050   FOR J=1  TO C2
1060   IF A(M3,J)>=P  THEN 1090
1070   S=J
1080   P=A(M3,J)
1090   NEXT J
1100   IF P=-.00001  THEN 1440
1110   GOSUB 1130
1120   GOSUB 1210
1125   GOTO 1040
1129   REM - NOW FIND WHICH VARIABLE LEAVE BASIS
1130   Q=1.E+38
1140   FOR I=1  TO M
1150   IF A(I,S)<=.00001  THEN 1190
1160   IF A(I,C1)/A(I,S)>=Q  THEN 1190
1170   R=I
1180   Q=A(I,C1)/A(I,S)
1190   NEXT I
1200   RETURN
1210   IF Q=1.E+38  THEN 1240
1220   GOSUB 1260
1230   RETURN
1240   PRINT "THE SOLUTION IS UNBOUNDED."
1250   GOTO 3060
1259   REM - PERFORM PIVOTING
1260   P=A(R,S)
1270   FOR I=1  TO M2
1280   IF I=R  THEN 1350
1290   FOR J=1  TO C1
1300   IF J=S  THEN 1340
1310   A(I,J)=A(I,J)-A(I,S)*A(R,J)/P
1320   IF ABS(A(I,J))>=.00001  THEN 1340
1330   A(I,J)=0
```

```
1340    NEXT J
1350    NEXT I
1360    FOR J=1  TO C1
1370    A(R,J)=A(R,J)/P
1380    NEXT J
1390    FOR I=1  TO M2
1400    A(I,S)=0
1410    NEXT I
1420    A(R,S)=1
1430    B(R)=S
1440    RETURN
2996    REM - *** DO THE FOLLOWING STEPS BEFORE RUNNING THE PROGRAM ***
2997    REM - TYPE IN COEFFICIENTS OF '<','=', AND '>' CONSTRAINTS IN
        DATA STATEMENTS STARTING AT LINE 3000, A SEPARATE DATA STATEMENT
        FOR EACH CONSTRAINT (LINES 3000 - 3030 IN OUR EXAMPLE)
2998    REM - TYPE IN CONSTANTS OF THE CONSTRAINTS IN A DATA STATEMENT
        FOLLOWING THE COEFFICIENT DATA, AND IN THE SAME ORDER AS THE CON
        STRAINT DATA WERE ENTERED (LINE 3040 IN OUR EXAMPLE)
2999    REM - TYPE IN THE COEFFICIENTS OF THE OBJECTIVE FUNCTION IN A
        DATA STATEMENT (LINE 3050 IN OUR EXAMPLE) FOLLOWING THE CONSTANTS
        DATA
3000    DATA 1,1,1,1,1
3010    DATA .9,.8,.95,.7,.3
3020    DATA .05,.05,.02,.3,.7
3030    DATA .05,.15,.03,0,0
3040    DATA 100,83,14,3
3050    DATA 6.13,7.12,5.85,4.57,3.96
3060    END
```

Matrix Addition, Subtraction, Scalar Multiplication

This program adds or subtracts two matrices, or multiplies a matrix by a given scalar. You must input the value of each element of each matrix. To perform addition or subtraction the dimensions of the two matrices must be equal.

The dimension of the matrices may be increased or decreased depending on the amount of memory available in your system. Statement 30 may be changed to:

$$30 \ DIM \ A(X,Y), \ B(X,Y)$$

where (X,Y) is your limit on the dimension of the matrices.

Example:

Find the sum of the following matrices, then multiply the resultant matrix by 3.

$$\begin{bmatrix} 1 & 0 & -1 \\ 5 & 8 & .5 \\ -1 & 2 & 0 \end{bmatrix} \quad \begin{bmatrix} -5 & -1 & 2 \\ 6 & -.1 & 0 \\ 3 & 4 & -2 \end{bmatrix}$$

```
:RUN
MATRIX ADDITION, SUBTRACTION, SCALAR MULTIPLICATION

1=ADDITION
2=SUBTRACTION
3=SCALAR MULTIPLICATION
WHICH OPERATION? 1
DIMENSION OF MATRIX (R,C)? 3,3
MATRIX 1:
ROW 1
VALUE COLUMN 1 ? 1
VALUE COLUMN 2 ? 0
VALUE COLUMN 3 ? -1
ROW 2
VALUE COLUMN 1 ? 5
VALUE COLUMN 2 ? 8
VALUE COLUMN 3 ? .5
ROW 3
VALUE COLUMN 1 ? -1
VALUE COLUMN 2 ? 2
VALUE COLUMN 3 ? 0
MATRIX 2:
ROW 1
VALUE COLUMN 1 ? -5
VALUE COLUMN 2 ? -1
VALUE COLUMN 3 ? 2
ROW 2
VALUE COLUMN 1 ? 6
VALUE COLUMN 2 ? -.1
VALUE COLUMN 3 ? 0
ROW 3
VALUE COLUMN 1 ? 3
```

```
VALUE COLUMN 2 ? 4
VALUE COLUMN 3 ? -2
-4     -1      1
 11     7.9     .5
  2      6     -2

MORE DATA? (1=YES,0=NO)? 1
WHICH OPERATION? 3
VALUE OF SCALAR? 3
DIMENSION OF MATRIX (R,C)? 3,3
MATRIX 1:
ROW 1
VALUE COLUMN 1 ? -4
VALUE COLUMN 2 ? -1
VALUE COLUMN 3 ? 1
ROW 2
VALUE COLUMN 1 ? 11
VALUE COLUMN 2 ? 7.9
VALUE COLUMN 3 ? .5
ROW 3
VALUE COLUMN 1 ? 2
VALUE COLUMN 2 ? 6
VALUE COLUMN 3 ? -2
-12     -3      3
 33     23.7    1.5
  6     18     -6

MORE DATA? (1=YES,0=NO)? 0

END PROGRAM



PROGRAM LISTING

  10   PRINT "MATRIX ADDITION, SUBTRACTION, SCALAR MULTIPLICATION"
  20   PRINT
  29   REM - ARRAYS SHOULD BE SET TO DIMENSIONS OF MATRICES
  30   DIM A(3,3), B(3,3)
  40   PRINT "1=ADDITION"
  50   PRINT "2=SUBTRACTION"
  60   PRINT "3=SCALAR MULTIPLICATION"
  69   REM - SELECT OPERATION BY ENTERING THE NUMBER (1-3) OF THE OPERATION
  70   PRINT "WHICH OPERATION";
  80   INPUT D
  89   REM - TEST FOR ADDITION OR SUBRACTION
  90   IF D<>3  THEN  120
 100   PRINT "VALUE OF SCALAR";
 110   INPUT S
 120   PRINT "DIMENSION OF MATRIX (R,C)";
 130   INPUT R,C
 138   REM - LOOP TO ENTER MATRIX VALUES
 139   REM - FOR SUBTRACTION, MATRIX 2 SUBTRACTED FROM MATRIX 1
 140   FOR K=1  TO 2
 150   IF K=2  THEN  180
 160   PRINT "MATRIX 1:"
 170   GOTO  190
 180   PRINT "MATRIX 2:"
```

```
190    FOR J=1   TO R
200    PRINT "ROW";J
210    FOR I=1   TO C
220    PRINT "VALUE COLUMN";I;
230    IF K=2   THEN   260
240    INPUT A(J,I)
250    GOTO   270
260    INPUT B(J,I)
270    NEXT I
280    NEXT J
289    REM - ONLY ONE MATRIX USED FOR SCALAR MULTIPLICATION
290    IF D=3   THEN   310
300    NEXT K
309    REM - STATEMENTS 310 TO 410 PERFORM REQUESTED OPERATION AND PRINT RES
       ULTANT MATRIX
310    FOR J=1   TO R
320    FOR I=1   TO C
330    IF D<>2   THEN   350
340    B(J,I)=-B(J,I)
350    IF D=3   THEN   380
360    PRINT A(J,I)+B(J,I);"   ";
370    GOTO   390
380    PRINT A(J,I)*S;"   ";
390    NEXT I
399    REM - ADVANCE OUTPUT DEVICE TO PRINT NEXT ROW
400    PRINT
410    NEXT J
420    PRINT
429    REM - RESTART OR END PROGRAM?
430    PRINT "MORE DATA? (1=YES,0=NO)";
440    INPUT D
450    IF D=1   THEN   70
460    END
```

Matrix Multiplication

This program multiplies two matrices. The first matrix is multiplied by the second. You must input the elements of each matrix.

In order for this operation to be performed the number of rows in the first matrix must equal the number of columns in the second matrix.

The dimensions of the matrices are presently limited to 10 x 10. This limit may be increased or decreased by altering line 30 according to the following scheme:

$$30 \ DIM \ A(X,Y), \ B(Z,X)$$

where: (X,Y) = dimension of matrix 1
(Z,X) = dimension of matrix 2

Example:

Multiply matrix 1 by matrix 2.

$$1 \begin{cases} 2 & -1 & 4 & 1 & 2 \\ 1 & 0 & 1 & 2 & -1 \\ 2 & 3 & -1 & 0 & -2 \end{cases}$$

$$2 \begin{cases} -2 & -1 & 2 \\ 0 & 2 & 1 \\ -1 & 1 & 4 \\ 3 & 0 & -1 \\ 2 & 1 & 2 \end{cases}$$

```
:30 DIM A(3,5), B(5,3)
:RUN
MATRIX MULTIPLICATION

DIMENSION OF MATRIX 1 (R,C)? 3,5
DIMENSION OF MATRIX 2 (R,C)? 5,3
MATRIX 1:
ROW 1
VALUE COLUMN 1 ? 2
VALUE COLUMN 2 ? -1
VALUE COLUMN 3 ? 4
VALUE COLUMN 4 ? 1
VALUE COLUMN 5 ? 2
ROW 2
VALUE COLUMN 1 ? 1
VALUE COLUMN 2 ? 0
VALUE COLUMN 3 ? 1
VALUE COLUMN 4 ? 2
VALUE COLUMN 5 ? -1
ROW 3
VALUE COLUMN 1 ? 2
VALUE COLUMN 2 ? 3
VALUE COLUMN 3 ? -1
VALUE COLUMN 4 ? 0
```

VALUE COLUMN 5 ? -2

MATRIX 2:
ROW 1
VALUE COLUMN 1 ? -2
VALUE COLUMN 2 ? -1
VALUE COLUMN 3 ? 2
ROW 2
VALUE COLUMN 1 ? 0
VALUE COLUMN 2 ? 2
VALUE COLUMN 3 ? 1
ROW 3
VALUE COLUMN 1 ? -1
VALUE COLUMN 2 ? 1
VALUE COLUMN 3 ? 4
ROW 4
VALUE COLUMN 1 ? 3
VALUE COLUMN 2 ? 0
VALUE COLUMN 3 ? -1
ROW 5
VALUE COLUMN 1 ? 2
VALUE COLUMN 2 ? 1
VALUE COLUMN 3 ? 2

```
-1     2    22
 1    -1     2
-7     1    -1
```

END PROGRAM

PROGRAM LISTING

```
 10   PRINT "MATRIX MULTIPLICATION"
 20   PRINT
 29   REM - ARRAYS A AND B SHOULD BE SET TO DIMENSIONS OF MATRICES
 30   DIM A(10,10), B(10,10)
 40   PRINT "DIMENSION OF MATRIX 1 (R,C)";
 50   INPUT R1,C1
 60   PRINT "DIMENSION OF MATRIX 2 (R,C)";
 70   INPUT R2,C2
 79   REM - # OF COLUMNS IN MATRIX 1 MUST EQUAL # OF ROWS IN MATRIX 2
 80   IF C1=R2   THEN   110
 90   PRINT "CANNOT BE MULTIPLIED; OTHER DIMENSIONS NECESSARY"
100   GOTO   40
109   REM - ENTER MATRIX VALUES
110   PRINT "MATRIX 1:"
120   FOR J=1   TO R1
130   PRINT "ROW";J
140   FOR I=1   TO C1
150   PRINT "VALUE COLUMN";I;
160   INPUT A(J,I)
170   NEXT I
180   NEXT J
190   PRINT
200   PRINT "MATRIX 2:"
210   FOR J=1   TO R2
```

```
220    PRINT "ROW";J
230    FOR I=1   TO C2
240    PRINT "VALUE COLUMN";I;
250    INPUT B(J,I)
260    NEXT I
270    NEXT J
280    PRINT
289    REM - PERFORM MATRIX MULTIPLICATION, PRINT RESULTANT MATRIX
290    FOR I=1   TO R1
300    FOR J=1   TO C2
310    S=0
320    FOR K=1   TO C1
330    S=S+A(I,K)*B(K,J)
340    NEXT K
350    PRINT S;"   ";
360    NEXT J
369    REM - ADVANCE OUTPUT DEVICE TO PRINT NEXT ROW
370    PRINT
380    NEXT I
390    END
```

Matrix Inversion

This program inverts a square matrix. The inversion is performed by a modified Gauss-Jordan elimination method.

The dimensions of the matrix are presently limited to 10 x 10. This limit may be increased or decreased by altering line 30 according to the following scheme:

$$30 \ DIM \ A(R,R), \ B(R,R)$$

where R = number of rows (or columns) in the matrix.

Example:

Invert matrix A.

$$A \begin{cases} 3 & 5 & -1 & -4 \\ 1 & 4 & -.7 & -3 \\ 0 & -2 & 0 & 1 \\ -2 & 6 & 0 & .3 \end{cases}$$

```
:RUN
MATRIX INVERSION

DIMENSION OF MATRIX? 4
MATRIX ELEMENTS:
ROW 1
VALUE COLUMN 1 ? 3
VALUE COLUMN 2 ? 5
VALUE COLUMN 3 ? -1
VALUE COLUMN 4 ? -4
ROW 2
VALUE COLUMN 1 ? 1
VALUE COLUMN 2 ? 4
VALUE COLUMN 3 ? -.7
VALUE COLUMN 4 ? -3
ROW 3
VALUE COLUMN 1 ? 0
VALUE COLUMN 2 ? -2
VALUE COLUMN 3 ? 0
VALUE COLUMN 4 ? 1
ROW 4
VALUE COLUMN 1 ? -2
VALUE COLUMN 2 ? 6
VALUE COLUMN 3 ? 0
VALUE COLUMN 4 ? .3

  .654   -.935   -.191    1.40000000E-02
  .198   -.283   -.103    .156
  .368   -1.955  -4.263   -.425
  .397   -.567    .793    .312

END PROGRAM
```

PROGRAM LISTING

```
10    PRINT "MATRIX INVERSION"
20    PRINT
29    REM - A() AND B() SHOULD BOTH BE SET TO THE DIMENSIONS OF THE MAT
   RIX
30    DIM A(10,10), B(10,10)
39    REM - MATRIX IS SQUARE SO ONLY ONE DIMENSION IS NEEDED
40    PRINT "DIMENSION OF MATRIX";
50    INPUT R
60    PRINT "MATRIX ELEMENTS:"
69    REM - ENTER MATRIX ELEMENTS
70    FOR J=1  TO R
80    PRINT "ROW";J
90    FOR I=1  TO R
100   PRINT "VALUE COLUMN";I;
110   INPUT A(J,I)
120   NEXT I
130   B(J,J)=1
140   NEXT J
149   REM - STATEMENTS 150 TO 420 INVERT MATRIX
150   FOR J=1  TO R
160   FOR I=J  TO R
170   IF A(I,J)<>0  THEN  210
180   NEXT I
190   PRINT "SINGULAR MATRIX"
200   GOTO  500
210   FOR K=1  TO R
220   S=A(J,K)
230   A(J,K)=A(I,K)
240   A(I,K)=S
250   S=B(J,K)
260   B(J,K)=B(I,K)
270   B(I,K)=S
280   NEXT K
290   T=1/A(J,J)
300   FOR K=1  TO R
310   A(J,K)=T*A(J,K)
320   B(J,K)=T*B(J,K)
330   NEXT K
340   FOR L=1  TO R
350   IF L=J  THEN  410
360   T=-A(L,J)
370   FOR K=1  TO R
380   A(L,K)=A(L,K)+T*A(J,K)
390   B(L,K)=B(L,K)+T*B(J,K)
400   NEXT K
410   NEXT L
420   NEXT J
430   PRINT
439   REM - PRINT RESULTANT MATRIX
440   FOR I=1  TO R
450   FOR J=1  TO R
459   REM - ROUND OFF, PRINT
460   PRINT INT(B(I,J)*1000+.5)/1000;" ";
470   NEXT J
479   REM - ADVANCE OUTPUT DEVICE TO PRINT NEXT LINE
480   PRINT
490   NEXT I
500   END
```

Permutations and Combinations

This program computes the number of permutations and combinations of *N* objects taken *D* at a time.

Examples:

How many permutations and combinations can be made of the 26 letters of the alphabet, taking five at a time?

How many different ways can 12 people sit on a bench if there is only room for two at a time?

```
:RUN
PERMUTATIONS AND COMBINATIONS

(ENTER 0 TO END PROGRAM)
TOTAL NUMBER OF OBJECTS? 26
SIZE OF SUBGROUP? 5
 7893600 PERMUTATIONS
 65780 COMBINATONS

TOTAL NUMBER OF OBJECTS? 12
SIZE OF SUBGROUP? 2
 132 PERMUTATIONS
 66 COMBINATONS

TOTAL NUMBER OF OBJECTS? 0

END PROGRAM
```

```
PROGRAM LISTING

   10   PRINT "PERMUTATIONS AND COMBINATIONS"
   20   PRINT
   30   PRINT "(ENTER 0 TO END PROGRAM)"
   40   PRINT "TOTAL NUMBER OF OBJECTS";
   50   INPUT N
   59   REM - TEST FOR END OF PROGRAM
   60   IF N=0  THEN  280
   70   PRINT "SIZE OF SUBGROUP";
   80   INPUT D
   89   REM - SIZE OF SUBGROUP CANNOT BE LARGER THAN SIZE OF GROUP
   90   IF D<=N  THEN  130
  100   PRINT "SUBGROUP TOO LARGE"
  110   PRINT
  120   GOTO  40
  129   REM - LINES 130 TO 200 COMPUTE PERMUTATIONS
  130   P=1
  140   C=1
  150   FOR I=N-D+1  TO N
  159   REM - DON'T ALLOW NUMBER SIZE TO OVERFLOW MACHINE CAPACITY
  160   IF 9.9E62/I>=P  THEN  190
  170   PRINT "MORE THAN 9.9E62 PERMUTATIONS"
```

```
180    GOTO  280
190    P=P*I
200    NEXT I
209    REM - COMPUTE INTERMEDIATE FACTORIAL FOR COMBINATIONS
210    FOR J=2  TO D
220    C=C*J
230    NEXT J
240    PRINT P;"PERMUTATIONS"
250    PRINT P/C;"COMBINATONS"
260    PRINT
269    REM - RESTART PROGRAM
270    GOTO   40
280    END
```

Mann-Whitney *U* Test

This program performs the Mann-Whitney *U* test on samples from two populations.

The dimension statement on line 30 limits the size of the samples. You can increase or decrease the dimension limits according to the following scheme:

$$30 \ \text{DIM} \ X(M), \ Y(N)$$

where: *M* = maximum size of first sample
N = maximum size of second sample

Example:

A group of ten women and a group of ten men were asked to rate the flavor of a frozen T.V. dinner on a scale of one to ten. The table below lists the scores. Count the number of times the women's scores are lower than the men's, and vice-versa.

women	1	3	4	3	6	8	9	7	8	4
men	7	9	8	5	10	9	10	6	5	2

```
:30 DIM X(10),Y(10)
:RUN
MANN-WHITNEY U-TEST

SAMPLE 1 :
  SIZE? 10
   DATA 1 ? 1
   DATA 2 ? 3
   DATA 3 ? 4
   DATA 4 ? 3
   DATA 5 ? 6
   DATA 6 ? 8
   DATA 7 ? 9
   DATA 8 ? 7
   DATA 9 ? 8
   DATA 10 ? 4

SAMPLE 2 :
  SIZE? 10
   DATA 1 ? 7
   DATA 2 ? 9
   DATA 3 ? 8
   DATA 4 ? 5
   DATA 5 ? 10
   DATA 6 ? 9
   DATA 7 ? 10
   DATA 8 ? 6
   DATA 9 ? 5
   DATA 10 ? 2

FIRST SAMPLE PRECEDING, U = 70
SECOND SAMPLE PRECEDING, U = 30

END PROGRAM
```

118

```
10    PRINT "MANN-WHITNEY U-TEST"
20    PRINT
29    REM - SET MAXIMUM SAMPLE SIZE TO X(M),Y(N)   (WHERE M=MAXIMUM SIZE O
   F SAMPLE 1, N=MAXIMUM SIZE OF SAMPLE 2)
30    DIM X(25),Y(25)
40    DIM N(2)
49    REM - INPUT THE TWO SAMPLES
50    FOR I=1   TO 2
60    PRINT "SAMPLE";I;"·"
70    PRINT "  SIZE";
80    INPUT N(I)
90    FOR J=1   TO N(I)
100   PRINT "   DATA";J;
110   INPUT Y(J)
120   NEXT J
129   REM - SORT EACH SAMPLE
130   FOR J=1   TO N(I)
140   FOR K=1   TO N(I)-J
150   C=Y(K)
170   IF Y(K)<Y(K+1)   THEN   200
180   Y(K)=Y(K+1)
190   Y(K+1)=C
200   NEXT K
210   NEXT J
220   PRINT
229   REM - TRANSFER FIRST SAMPLE TO X-ARRAY
230   IF I=2   THEN   270
240   FOR J=1   TO N(1)
250   X(J)=Y(J)
260   NEXT J
270   NEXT I
279   REM - ADD UP RANKS
280   R=1
290   I=0
300   J=0
310   I=I+1
320   J=J+1
330   IF I>N(1)   THEN   580
340   IF J>N(2)   THEN   620
350   IF X(I)<Y(J)   THEN   620
360   IF Y(J)<X(I)   THEN   590
369   REM - LINES 370-570 HANDLE EQUAL SCORES FROM BOTH SAMPLES
370   K=2
380   M=I
390   L=J
400   R1=2*R+1
410   R=R+2
420   I=I+1
430   J=J+1
440   IF I>N(1)   THEN   480
450   IF X(I)<>X(I-1)   THEN   480
460   I=I+1
470   GOTO   510
480   IF J>N(2)   THEN   550
```

```
490    IF Y(J)<>Y(J-1)   THEN   550
500    J=J+1
510    R1=R1+R
520    R=R+1
530    K=K+1
540    GOTO   440
550    X=X+(I-M)*R1/K
560    Y=Y+(J-L)*R1/K
570    GOTO   330
580    IF J>N(2)   THEN   660
590    Y=Y+R
600    J=J+1
610    GOTO   640
620    X=X+R
630    I=I+1
640    R=R+1
650    GOTO   330
659    REM - U1=NUMBER OF·TIMES SAMPLE 1 SCORES PRECEDE SAMPLE 2 SCORES
660    U1=N(1)*N(2)+N(1)*(N(1)+1)/2-X
669    REM - U2=NUMBER OF·TIMES SAMPLE 2 SCORES PRECEDE SAMPLE 1 SCORES
670    U2=N(1)*N(2)+N(2)*(N(2)+1)/2-Y
680    PRINT
690    PRINT "FIRST SAMPLE PRECEDING, U =";U1
700    PRINT "SECOND SAMPLE PRECEDING, U =";U2
710    END
```

Mean, Variance, Standard Deviation

This program calculates the arithmetic mean, variance and standard deviation of grouped or ungrouped data. The data may represent the entire population or just a sample.

Examples:

There are ten people in a hotel lobby, aged 87, 53, 35, 42, 9, 48, 51, 60, 39 and 44. What would the mean, variance and standard deviation of the ages of all the people in the hotel be using the people in the lobby as a sample?

Find the mean, variance and standard deviation of the ages of the cream cheese on a market shelf. The table below lists the age distribution of 50 packages. Assume the table shows the store's entire inventory. What if it is only a sample of the inventory?

age	1	2	3	4	5	6
quantity	15	10	9	6	7	3

cream cheese

```
:RUN
MEAN, VARIANCE, STANDARD DEVIATION

WHICH METHOD (0=POPULATION,1=SAMPLE)? 1
KIND OF DATA (0=GROUPED,1=UNGROUPED)? 1
NUMBER OF OBSERVATIONS? 10
ITEM 1 ? 87
ITEM 2 ? 53
ITEM 3 ? 35
ITEM 4 ? 42
ITEM 5 ? 9
ITEM 6 ? 48
ITEM 7 ? 51
ITEM 8 ? 60
ITEM 9 ? 39
ITEM 10 ? 44

MEAN            VARIANCE         STANDARD DEVIATION
 46.8            389.7333333333   19.741664908

MORE DATA (1=YES, 0=NO)? 1

WHICH METHOD (0=POPULATION,1=SAMPLE)? 0
KIND OF DATA (0=GROUPED,1=UNGROUPED)? 0
NUMBER OF OBSERVATIONS? 6
ITEM, FREQUENCY 1 ? 1,15
ITEM, FREQUENCY 2 ? 2,10
ITEM, FREQUENCY 3 ? 3,9
ITEM, FREQUENCY 4 ? 4,6
ITEM, FREQUENCY 5 ? 5,7
ITEM, FREQUENCY 6 ? 6,3

MEAN            VARIANCE         STANDARD DEVIATION
 2.78            2.5716           1.6036209028
```

```
MORE DATA (1=YES, 0=NO)? 1

WHICH METHOD (0=POPULATION,1=SAMPLE)? 1
KIND OF DATA (0=GROUPED,1=UNGROUPED)? 0
NUMBER OF OBSERVATIONS? 6
ITEM, FREQUENCY 1 ? 1,15
ITEM, FREQUENCY 2 ? 2,10
ITEM, FREQUENCY 3 ? 3,9
ITEM, FREQUENCY 4 ? 4,6
ITEM, FREQUENCY 5 ? 5,7
ITEM, FREQUENCY 6 ? 6,3

MEAN              VARIANCE        STANDARD DEVIATION
 2.78             2.624081632653  1.6199017355

MORE DATA (1=YES, 0=NO)? 0

END PROGRAM


PROGRAM LISTING

  10    PRINT "MEAN, VARIANCE, STANDARD DEVIATION"
  20    PRINT
  30    PRINT "WHICH METHOD (0=POPULATION,1=SAMPLE)";
  40    INPUT S
  50    PRINT "KIND OF DATA (0=GROUPED,1=UNGROUPED)";
  60    INPUT K
  70    PRINT "NUMBER OF OBSERVATIONS";
  80    INPUT N
  90    R=0
 100    M=0
 110    P=0
 120    IF K=1  THEN  230
 129    REM - FOR GROUPED DATA
 130    FOR I=1  TO N
 140    PRINT "ITEM, FREQUENCY";I;
 150    INPUT A,B
 159    REM - ACCUMULATE ENTERED VALUES
 160    R=R+B*A
 169    REM - ACCUMULATE INTERMEDIATE VALUES FOR VARIANCE
 170    P=P+B
 180    M=M+B*A↑2
 190    NEXT I
 199    REM - CALCULATE MEAN AND VARIANCE
 200    R=R/P
 210    V=(M-P*R↑2)/(P-S)
 219    REM - PRINT RESULTS
 220    GOTO  310
 229    REM - FOR UNGROUPED DATA
 230    FOR I=1  TO N
 240    PRINT "ITEM";I;
 250    INPUT D
 259    REM - ACCUMULATE ENTERED VALUES
 260    P=P+D
 269    REM - ACCUMULATE INTERMEDIATE VALUES FOR VARIANCE
 270    M=M+D↑2
```

```
280    NEXT I
289    REM - CALCULATE MEAN AND VARIANCE, PRINT
290    R=P/N
300    V=(M-N*R↑2)/(N-S)
310    PRINT
319    REM - PRINT RESULTS
320    PRINT "MEAN","VARIANCE","STANDARD DEVIATION"
330    PRINT R,V,SQR(V)
340    PRINT
349    REM - RESTART OR END PROGRAM?
350    PRINT "MORE DATA (1=YES, 0=NO)";
360    INPUT S
370    IF S=1   THEN    20
380    END
```

Geometric Mean and Deviation

This program computes the geometric mean and standard deviation of a set of data.

Example:

Find the geometric mean and standard deviation of 3, 5, 8, 3, 7, 2.

```
:RUN
GEOMETRIC MEAN AND DEVIATION

(TO END PROGRAM ENTER 0 OBSERVATIONS)
NUMBER OF OBSERVATIONS? 6
ITEM 1 ? 3
ITEM 2 ? 5
ITEM 3 ? 8
ITEM 4 ? 3
ITEM 5 ? 7
ITEM 6 ? 2
GEOMETRIC MEAN = 4.140680833732
GEOMETRIC DEVIATION = 1.723689564961

NUMBER OF OBSERVATIONS? 0

END PROGRAM


PROGRAM LISTING

    10    PRINT "GEOMETRIC MEAN AND DEVIATION"
    20    PRINT
    30    PRINT "(TO END PROGRAM ENTER 0 OBSERVATIONS)"
    40    PRINT "NUMBER OF OBSERVATIONS";
    50    INPUT N
    59    REM - TEST FOR END OF PROGRAM
    60    IF N=0  THEN  200
    69    REM - COMPUTE WHICH ROOT TO USE
    70    P=1/N
    80    M=1
    90    FOR I=1  TO N
   100    PRINT "ITEM";I;
   110    INPUT D
   119    REM - ITERATIVELY COMPUTE MEAN
   120    M=M*D↑P
   129    REM - ACCUMULATE  INTERMEDIATE TERM FOR DEVIATION
   130    Q=Q+LOG(D)↑2
   140    NEXT I
   149    REM - COMPUTE DEVIATION
   150    R=EXP(SQR(Q/(N-1)-(N/(N-1)*(LOG(M))↑2)))
   160    PRINT "GEOMETRIC MEAN =";M
   170    PRINT "GEOMETRIC DEVIATION =";R
   180    PRINT
   189    REM - RESTART PROGRAM
   190    GOTO    40
   200    END
```

Binomial Distribution

This program calculates the probability of obtaining a given number of successes in a given number of Bernoulli trials. You must provide the probability of success on a single trial.

Examples:

What is the probability of getting three heads in five tosses of a fair coin?

What is the probability that in five rolls of a fair die, a one (1) appears twice?

```
:RUN
BINOMIAL DISTRIBUTION

(TO END PROGRAM ENTER 0)
NUMBER OF TRIALS? 5
EXACT NUMBER OF SUCCESSES? 3
PROBABILITY OF SUCCESS? .5
PROBABILITY OF 3 SUCCESSES IN 5 TRIALS = .3124999999998

NUMBER OF TRIALS? 5
EXACT NUMBER OF SUCCESSES? 2
PROBABILITY OF SUCCESS? .166666667
PROBABILITY OF 2 SUCCESSES IN 5 TRIALS = .1607510292571

NUMBER OF TRIALS? 0

END PROGRAM
```

PROGRAM LISTING

```
10    PRINT "BINOMIAL DISTRIBUTION"
20    PRINT
30    DIM M(3)
40    PRINT "(TO END PROGRAM ENTER 0)"
50    PRINT "NUMBER OF TRIALS";
60    INPUT N
70    IF N=0  THEN  270
80    PRINT "EXACT NUMBER OF SUCCESSES";
90    INPUT X
100   PRINT "PROBABILITY OF SUCCESS";
110   INPUT P
119   REM - COMPUTE THE FACTORIALS
120   M(1)=N
130   M(2)=X
140   M(3)=N-X
150   FOR I=1  TO 3
160   IF M(I)=0  THEN  220
170   A=1
180   FOR J=1  TO M(I)
190   A=A*J
200   NEXT J
210   M(I)=LOG(A)
```

```
220   NEXT I
229   REM - USING THE COMPUTED FACTORIALS, COMPUTE PROBABILITY
230   R=EXP(M(1)-M(2)-M(3)+X*LOG(P)+(N-X)*LOG(1-P))
240   PRINT "PROBABILITY OF";X;"SUCCESSES IN";N;"TRIALS =";R
250   PRINT
260   GOTO    50
270   END
```

Poisson Distribution

Using the Poisson distribution this program calculates the probability of an event occurring a given number of times. You must know the expected frequency of the event.

Example:

2000 people are injected with a serum. The probability of any one person having a bad reaction is .001. Thus we can expect two (.001•2000=2) individuals will suffer a bad reaction. What is the probability that four people will have bad reactions? Only one person?

```
:RUN
POISSON DISTRIBUTION

(TO END PROGRAM ENTER 0)
CALCULATED FREQUENCY? 2
TEST FREQUENCY? 4
PROBABILITY OF 4 OCCURRENCES = 9.02235221E-02

CALCULATED FREQUENCY? 2
TEST FREQUENCY? 1
PROBABILITY OF 1 OCCURRENCES = .270670566473

CALCULATED FREQUENCY? 0

END PROGRAM


PROGRAM LISTING

 10   PRINT "POISSON DISTRIBUTION"
 20   PRINT
 30   PRINT "(TO END PROGRAM ENTER 0)"
 40   PRINT "CALCULATED FREQUENCY";
 50   INPUT L
 59   REM - END PROGRAM?
 60   IF L=0  THEN  180
 70   PRINT "TEST FREQUENCY";
 80   INPUT X
 89   REM - COMPUTE FACTORIAL
 90   A=1
100   FOR I=1  TO X
110   A=A*I
120   NEXT I
129   REM - COMPUTE PROBABILITY
130   A=LOG(A)
140   A=EXP(-L+X*LOG(L)-A)
150   PRINT "PROBABILITY OF";X;"OCCURRENCES =";A
160   PRINT
169   REM - RESTART PROGRAM
170   GOTO   40
180   END
```

Normal Distribution

This program calculates the probability and frequency of given values on a standard normal distribution curve. You can use non-standard variables if you know the mean and standard deviation.

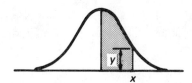

Standard normal distribution

The shaded area represents the probability of x. y corresponds to the frequency of x.

The normal probability is approximated using the following formula:

$$\text{probability} = 1 - r(a_1 t + a_2 t^2 + a_3 t^3) + \epsilon(x)$$

$$\text{where:} \quad a_1 = .4361836$$
$$a_2 = -.1201676$$
$$a_3 = .9372980$$
$$r = (e^{-x^2/2})(2\pi)^{-1/2}$$
$$t = (1 + .3326x)^{-1}$$
$$|\epsilon(x)| < 10^{-5}$$

Example:

The mean weight of the male students at a college is 150 pounds. The standard deviation is 15 pounds. If the weights are normally distributed, what is the probability that a student weighs between 150 and 180 pounds? Between 130 and 150 pounds?

```
:RUN
NORMAL DISTRIBUTION

(0=STANDARD, 1=NON-STANDARD)
WHICH TYPE OF VARIABLE? 1
MEAN? 150
STANDARD DEVIATION? 15

TO END PROGRAM ENTER X=99999
X =? 180
FREQUENCY = 5.39909665E-02
PROBABILITY = .977241189885

X =? 130
FREQUENCY = .1640100746762
PROBABILITY = .908798074993

X =? 99999

END PROGRAM
```

```
 10    PRINT "NORMAL DISTRIBUTION"
 20    PRINT
 30    PRINT "(0=STANDARD, 1=NON-STANDARD)"
 40    PRINT "WHICH TYPE OF VARIABLE";
 50    INPUT S
 60    IF S=0  THEN  120
 69    REM - LINES 70-110 REQUEST 'NON-STANDARD' VARIABLE DATA
 70    PRINT "MEAN";
 80    INPUT M
 90    PRINT "STANDARD DEVIATION";
100    INPUT S
110    GOTO  130
120    S=1
130    PRINT
140    PRINT "TO END PROGRAM ENTER X=99999"
150    PRINT "X =";
160    INPUT Y
170    IF Y=99999  THEN  290
179    REM - ADJUST FOR NON-STANDARD VARIABLES
180    Y=ABS((Y-M)/S)
189    REM - COMPUTE FREQUENCY (Y COORDINATE)
190    R=EXP(-(Y↑2)/2)/2.5066282746
200    PRINT "FREQUENCY =";R
210    Z=Y
219    REM - APPROXIMATE PROBABILITY (AREA UNDER CURVE)
220    Y=1/(1+.33267*ABS(Y))
230    T=1-R*(.4361836*Y-.1201676*Y↑2+.937298*Y↑3)
239    REM - ADJUST FOR NEGATIVE VARIABLES
240    IF Z>=0  THEN  260
250    T=1-T
260    PRINT "PROBABILITY =";T
270    PRINT
280    GOTO  150
290    END
```

Chi-square Distribution

This program calculates the tail-end value for points on a chi-square (X^2) distribution curve. You must provide the value of X^2 and the degrees of freedom.

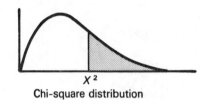

Chi-square distribution

The shaded area represents the tail-end value of X^2.

The X^2 distribution function is calculated using the following formulas:

$$\text{with } v \text{ odd, tail-end value} = 1 - \frac{(X^2)^{(v+1)/2} \cdot e^{-x^2/2}}{1 \cdot 3 \cdot 5 \ldots \cdot v} \cdot \left(\frac{2}{X^2 \pi}\right)^{1/2} \cdot Z$$

$$\text{with } v \text{ even, tail-end value} = 1 - \frac{(X^2)^{v/2} \cdot e^{-x^2/2}}{2 \cdot 4 \cdot \ldots v} \cdot Z$$

where: v = degrees of freedom

$$Z = 1 + \sum_{m=1}^{\infty} \frac{(X^2)^m}{(v+2) \cdot (v+4) \cdot \ldots (v+2m)}$$

Since the summation in the calculation of Z cannot actually extend to infinity, we stop summation when the next term is less than a chosen level of precision. The computational precision is limited to approximately 10^{-7}.

Example:

Of a group of 168 people who complained they did not sleep well, 54 were given sleeping pills and the remainder received placebos. They were later asked whether or not the pills had helped them sleep. The X^2 statistic for this study was computed to be 2.571108 with one degree of freedom. What is the tail-end value?

```
:RUN
CHI-SQUARE DISTRIBUTION

(TO END PROGRAM ENTER 0)
DEGREES OF FREEDOM? 1
CHI-SQUARE? 2.571108
TAIL END VALUE = .108831484618

DEGREES OF FREEDOM? 0

END PROGRAM
```

PROGRAM LISTING

```
10    PRINT "CHI-SQUARE DISTRIBUTION"
20    PRINT
30    PRINT "(TO END PROGRAM ENTER 0)"
40    PRINT "DEGREES OF FREEDOM";
50    INPUT V
60    IF V=0   THEN  280
70    PRINT "CHI-SQUARE";
80    INPUT W
89    REM - R=THE DENOMINATOR PRODUCT
90    R=1
100   FOR I=V  TO 2  STEP -2
110   R=R*I
120   NEXT I
129   REM - K=THE NUMERATOR PRODUCT
130   K=W↑(INT((V+1)/2))*EXP(-W/2)/R
139   REM - THE PI FACTOR IS USED ONLY WHEN DEG. FREEDOM ARE ODD
140   IF INT(V/2)=V/2   THEN  170
150   J=SQR(2/W/3.141592653599)
160   GOTO  180
169   REM - L (SUMMATION FACTOR) CALCULATED LINES 170-240
170   J=1
180   L=1
190   M=1
200   V=V+2
210   M=M*W/V
219   REM - CHECK FOR END OF SUMMATION
220   IF M<.0000001   THEN  250
230   L=L+M
240   GOTO  200
250   PRINT "TAIL END VALUE =";1-J*K*L
260   PRINT
270   GOTO    40
280   END
```

OPTION

You may wish to compute the percentile rather than the tail-end value. This value corresponds to the unshaded area in the figure above. The program changes necessary are listed following the example below.

Example:

What is the percentile in the example above?

```
:RUN
CHI-SQUARE DISTRIBUTION

(TO END PROGRAM ENTER 0)
DEGREES OF FREEDOM? 1
CHI-SQUARE? 2.571108
PERCENTILE = .8911685153823

DEGREES OF FREEDOM? 0

END PROGRAM
```

PROGRAM LISTING

```
    1    REM - OPTION 250
   10    PRINT "CHI-SQUARE DISTRIBUTION"
    .
    .
    .
  240    GOTO  200
  250    PRINT "PERCENTILE =";J*K*L
  260    PRINT
  270    GOTO   40
  280    END
```

Chi-square Test

This program calculates the chi-square (X^2) statistic and degrees of freedom associated with a given contingency table. The expected value for each cell and X^2 contribution from each cell are also printed.

The dimension statement at line 30 limits the size of the contingency table. You can change the dimensions according to the following scheme:

$$30 \text{ DIM } V1(R \cdot C), V2(C), A(R)$$

where:
R = number of rows in the contingency table
C = number of columns in the contingency table

Example:

Of a group of people who complained they could not sleep well, some were given sleeping pills while others were given placebos. Later they were asked whether or not the pills had helped them sleep. The results are detailed in the table below. What is the value of the X^2 statistic?

	slept well	slept poorly
sleeping pill	44	10
placebo	81	35

```
:30 DIM V1(4),V2(2),A(2)
:RUN
CHI-SQUARE TEST

NUMBER OF ROWS? 2
NUMBER OF COLUMNS? 2
CONTINGENCY TABLE:
ROW 1
   ELEMENT 1 ? 44
   ELEMENT 2 ? 10
ROW 2
   ELEMENT 1 ? 81
   ELEMENT 2 ? 35

OBSERVED VALUE    EXPECTED VALUE    CHI↑2 CONTRIBUTION
   COLUMN 1
      44             39.70588235294    .3625490196148
      81             85.29411764706    .1687728194759
   COLUMN 2
      10             14.29411764706   1.007080610041
      35             30.70588235294    .468813387433

CHI-SQUARE = 2.007215836564
DEGREES OF FREEDOM = 1
```

```
 10    PRINT "CHI-SQUARE TEST"
 20    PRINT
 28    REM - LIMIT SIZE OF CONTINGENCY TABLES TO V1(R*C),V2(C),A(R)
 29    REM - WHERE R=NO. OF ROWS, C=NO. OF COLUMNS
 30    DIM V1(25),V2(5),A(5)
 40    PRINT "NUMBER OF ROWS";
 49    REM - LINES 50-150 INPUT CONTINGENCY TABLE
 50    INPUT R
 60    PRINT "NUMBER OF COLUMNS";
 70    INPUT C
 80    PRINT "CONTINGENCY TABLE:"
 90    FOR I=1   TO R
100    PRINT "ROW";I
110    FOR J=1   TO C
120    PRINT "   ELEMENT";J;
130    INPUT V1((I-1)*C+J)
140    NEXT J
150    NEXT I
160    PRINT
169    REM - ADD UP MARGINAL FREQUENCIES FOR EACH ROW
170    L=0
180    M=1
190    FOR I=1   TO R
200    FOR J=1   TO C
210    A(I)=A(I)+V1(M)
220    M=M+1
230    NEXT J
240    L=L+A(I)
250    NEXT I
260    N=R*C
269    REM - ADD UP MARGINAL FREQUENCIES FOR EACH COLUMN
270    FOR I=1   TO C
280    FOR J=I   TO N  STEP C
290    V2(I)=V2(I)+V1(J)
300    NEXT J
310    NEXT I
320    Z=0
330    PRINT "OBSERVED VALUE","EXPECTED VALUE","CHI↑2 CONTRIBUTION"
340    FOR I=1   TO C
350    PRINT "   COLUMN";I
360    FOR J=1   TO R
369    REM - P=EXPECTED CELL VALUE
370    P=A(J)*V2(I)/L
375    X=I+(J-1)*C
379    REM  - USE YATES' CORRECTION FOR CONTINUITY IN 2 X 2 CHI-SQUARE
       TESTS
380    IF R<>2   THEN   390
381    IF  C<>2   THEN   390
382    Y=(ABS(V1(X)-P)-.5)↑2/P
383    GOTO  400
389    REM - Y=CHI-SQUARE CONTRIBUTION FROM THIS CELL
390    Y=(V1(X)-P)↑2/P
399    REM - Z=TOTAL CHI-SQUARE VALUE
400    Z=Z+Y
410    PRINT "       ";V1(X),P,Y
420    NEXT J
430    NEXT I
440    PRINT
450    PRINT "CHI-SQUARE =";Z
460    PRINT "DEGREES OF FREEDOM =";(C-1)*(R-1)
470    END
```

Student's t-distribution

This program calculates right-tail values for points on a t-distribution curve. You must provide the value of t and the degrees of freedom.

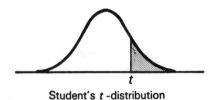

Student's t-distribution

The shaded area represents the right-tail value for t.

The right-tail value is approximated using the following formula:

$$\text{right-tail value} = \frac{1}{4}(1 + a_1 x + a_2 x^2 + a_3 x^3 + a_4 x^4)^{-4} + \epsilon(x)$$

where: a_1 = .196854
a_2 = .115194
a_3 = .000344
a_4 = .019527
$x = \left(t^{2/3}\left(1 - \frac{2}{9d}\right) - \frac{7}{9}\right)\left(\frac{2}{9} + t^{4/3} \cdot \frac{2}{9d}\right)^{-1/2}$
d = degrees of freedom

$$|\epsilon(x)| < 2.5 \cdot 10^{-4}$$

Examples:

What is the right-tail value when the t-value is 2.921 and there are 16 degrees of freedom?

What is the right-tail value when the t-value is 11.178 and there are 5 degrees of freedom?

```
:RUN
STUDENT'S T-DISTRIBUTION

(TO END PROGRAM ENTER A T-VALUE OF 0)
T-VALUE? 2.921
DEGREES OF FREEDOM? 16
RIGHT TAIL VALUE = 4.90000000E-03

T-VALUE? 11.178
DEGREES OF FREEDOM? 5
RIGHT TAIL VALUE = 2.00000000E-04

T-VALUE? 0

END PROGRAM
```

```
10    PRINT "STUDENT'S T-DISTRIBUTION"
20    PRINT
30    PRINT "(TO END PROGRAM ENTER A T-VALUE OF 0)"
40    PRINT "T-VALUE";
50    INPUT T
60    IF T=0   THEN   340
70    PRINT "DEGREES OF FREEDOM";
80    INPUT D
90    X=1
100   Y=1
110   T=T↑2
119   REM - COMPUTE USING INVERSE FOR SMALL T-VALUES
120   IF T<1   THEN   170
130   S=Y
140   R=D
150   Z=T
160   GOTO   200
170   S=D
180   R=Y
190   Z=1/T
200   J=2/9/S
210   K=2/9/R
219   REM - COMPUTE USING APPROXIMATION FORMULAS
220   L=ABS((1-K)*Z↑(1/3)-1+J)/SQR(K*Z↑(2/3)+J)
230   IF R<4   THEN   270
240   X=.25/(1+L*(.196854+L*(.115194+L*(.000344+L*.019527))))↑4
250   X=INT(X*10000+.5)/10000
260   GOTO   290
270   L=L*(1+.08*L↑4/R↑3)
280   GOTO   240
289   REM - ADJUST IF INVERSE WAS COMPUTED
290   IF T>=1   THEN   310
300   X=1-X
310   PRINT "RIGHT TAIL VALUE =";X
320   PRINT
330   GOTO    40
340   END
```

Student's *t*- distribution Test

This program calculates the *t*-statistic and degrees of freedom for Student's distribution. The calculations can be based on any one of three hypotheses.

The first hypothesis assumes that one population mean is equal to a given value. You must enter the elements of the sample and the value of the mean.

The remaining hypotheses compare two populations. In both tests the means of the two populations are equal, but the standard deviations may be equal or unequal. For these hypotheses you must enter the elements of each sample.

The dimension statement at line 30 limits the size of the samples you may enter. You can change the limit according to the following scheme:

```
30 DIM P(N,2)
```

where *N* = maximum sample size.

Examples:

A sample of children's IQ's was taken, the results being 101, 99, 120, 79, 111, 98, 106, 112, 87, and 97. Calculate the *t*-statistic assuming the population mean is 100.

A second sample was taken, the results being 101, 95, 130, 150, 75, 79, 111, 100, 98 and 91. Calculate the *t*-statistic based on the hypothesis that the two samples have equal means and standard deviations.

```
:RUN
STUDENT'S T-DISTRIBUTION TEST

TEST 1: MEAN=X
TEST 2: MEAN=MEAN,STANDARD DEVIATION=STANDARD DEVIATION
TEST 3: MEAN=MEAN,STANDARD DEVIATION<>STANDARD DEVIATION
WHICH HYPOTHESIS? 1

SAMPLE 1 :
  NUMBER OF ELEMENTS? 10
    ELEMENT 1 ? 101
    ELEMENT 2 ? 99
    ELEMENT 3 ? 120
    ELEMENT 4 ? 79
    ELEMENT 5 ? 111
    ELEMENT 6 ? 98
    ELEMENT 7 ? 106
    ELEMENT 8 ? 112
    ELEMENT 9 ? 87
    ELEMENT 10 ? 97

VALUE OF MEAN? 100

T-VALUE = .26151301641
DEGREES OF FREEDOM = 9

END PROGRAM
```

```
:RUN
STUDENT'S T-DISTRIBUTION TEST

TEST 1: MEAN=X
TEST 2: MEAN=MEAN,STANDARD DEVIATION=STANDARD DEVIATION
TEST 3: MEAN=MEAN,STANDARD DEVIATION<>STANDARD DEVIATION
WHICH HYPOTHESIS? 2

SAMPLE 1 :
  NUMBER OF ELEMENTS? 10
    ELEMENT 1 ? 101
    ELEMENT 2 ? 99
    ELEMENT 3 ? 120
    ELEMENT 4 ? 79
    ELEMENT 5 ? 111
    ELEMENT 6 ? 98
    ELEMENT 7 ? 106
    ELEMENT 8 ? 112
    ELEMENT 9 ? 87
    ELEMENT 10 ? 97
SAMPLE 2 :
  NUMBER OF ELEMENTS? 10
    ELEMENT 1 ? 101
    ELEMENT 2 ? 95
    ELEMENT 3 ? 130
    ELEMENT 4 ? 150
    ELEMENT 5 ? 75
    ELEMENT 6 ? 79
    ELEMENT 7 ? 111
    ELEMENT 8 ? 100
    ELEMENT 9 ? 98
    ELEMENT 10 ? 91


T-VALUE = .246515212849
DEGREES OF FREEDOM = 18

END PROGRAM


PROGRAM LISTING

   10    PRINT "STUDENT'S T-DISTRIBUTION TEST"
   20    PRINT
   29    REM - LIMIT SAMPLE SIZE TO P(N,2)  WHERE N=MAX. SAMPLE SIZE
   30    DIM P(10,2)
   40    DIM V(2),R(2),M(2),D(2)
   50    PRINT "TEST 1: MEAN=X"
   60    PRINT "TEST 2: MEAN=MEAN,STANDARD DEVIATION=STANDARD DEVIATION"
   70    PRINT "TEST 3: MEAN=MEAN,STANDARD DEVIATION<>STANDARD DEVIATION"
   80    PRINT "WHICH HYPOTHESIS";
   90    INPUT T
  100    PRINT
  109    REM - INPUT 1 OR 2 SAMPLES DEPENDING ON HYPOTHESIS
  110    FOR I=1  TO SGN(T-1)+1
  120    V(I)=0
  130    D(I)=0
```

```
140    PRINT "SAMPLE";I;":"
150    PRINT "   NUMBER OF ELEMENTS";
160    INPUT R(I)
170    FOR J=1  TO R(I)
180    PRINT "    ELEMENT";J;
190    INPUT P(J,I)
199    REM - ACCUMULATE SAMPLES
200    V(I)=V(I)+P(J,I)
210    D(I)=D(I)+P(J,I)↑2
220    NEXT J
229    REM - COMPUTE INTERMEDIATE VALUES
230    M(I)=V(I)/R(I)
240    V(I)=(D(I)-V(I)↑2/R(I))/(R(I)-1)
250    NEXT I
260    PRINT
270    IF T=2  THEN  340
280    IF T=3  THEN  380
289    REM - INPUT GIVEN VALUE FOR FIRST HYPOTHESIS
290    PRINT "VALUE OF MEAN";
300    INPUT M
309    REM - COMPUTE T AND DEGREES OF FREEDOM FOR FIRST HYPOTHESIS
310    A=(M(1)-M)*SQR(R(1)/V(1))
320    B=R(1)-1
330    GOTO  420
339    REM - COMPUTE T AND DEGREES OF FREEDOM FOR SECOND HYPOTHESIS
340    A=(M(1)-M(2))/SQR(1/R(1)+1/R(2))
350    B=R(1)+R(2)-2
360    A=A/SQR(((R(1)-1)*V(1)+(R(2)-1)*V(2))/B)
370    GOTO  420
379    REM - COMPUTE T AND DEGREES OF FREEDOM FOR THIRD HYPOTHESIS
380    A=(M(1)-M(2))/SQR(V(1)/R(1)+V(2)/R(2))
390    B=(V(1)/R(1)+V(2)/R(2))↑2
400    B=B/((V(1)/R(1))↑2/(R(1)+1)+(V(2)/R(2))↑2/(R(2)+1))-2
410    B=INT(B+.5)
420    PRINT
430    PRINT "T-VALUE =";ABS(A)
440    PRINT "DEGREES OF FREEDOM =";B
450    END
```

F -distribution

This program calculates percentile values for given values on an *F* -distribution curve. You must provide the value of *F,* the degrees of freedom in the numerator and the degrees of freedom in the denominator.

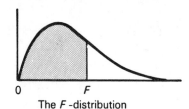

The *F* -distribution

The area of the shaded region represents the percentile.

The *F* -distribution function is approximated using the following formula:

$$\text{percentile} = 1 - \frac{1}{2}(1 + a_1 y + a_2 y^2 + a_3 y^3 + a_4 y^4)^{-4} + \epsilon(y)$$

where:
$$a_1 = .196854$$
$$a_2 = .115194$$
$$a_3 = .000344$$
$$a_4 = .019527$$
$$y = (F^{1/3}(1 - \frac{2}{9d_2}) - (1 - \frac{2}{9d_1}))(\frac{2}{9d_1} + F^{2/3} \cdot \frac{2}{9d_2}) - 1/2$$
$$d_1 = \text{degrees of freedom in numerator}$$
$$d_2 = \text{degrees of freedom in denominator}$$
$$|\epsilon(y)| < 2.5 \times 10^{-4}$$

Examples:

What is the percentile on an *F* -distribution curve when the *F* -value is .474 and the degrees of freedom are 1 and 18?

What is the percentile when the *F* -value is 23.7 and the degrees of freedom are 3 and 6?

```
:RUN
F-DISTRIBUTION

(TO END PROGRAM ENTER AN F-VALUE OF 0)
F-VALUE? .474
DEGREES OF FREEDOM IN NUMERATOR? 1
DEGREES OF FREEDOM IN DENOMINATOR? 18
PERCENTILE = .4937

F-VALUE? 23.7
DEGREES OF FREEDOM IN NUMERATOR? 3
DEGREES OF FREEDOM IN DENOMINATOR? 6
PERCENTILE = .9984

F-VALUE? 0

END PROGRAM
```

```
10    PRINT "F-DISTRIBUTION"
20    PRINT
30    PRINT "(TO END PROGRAM ENTER AN F-VALUE OF 0)"
40    PRINT "F-VALUE";
50    INPUT F
60    IF F=0  THEN  340
70    PRINT "DEGREES OF FREEDOM IN NUMERATOR";
80    INPUT D1
90    PRINT "DEGREES OF FREEDOM IN DENOMINATOR";
100   INPUT D2
110   X=1
119   REM - COMPUTE USING INVERSE FOR SMALL F-VALUES
120   IF F<1  THEN  170
130   S=D1
140   T=D2
150   Z=F
160   GOTO  200
170   S=D2
180   T=D1
190   Z=1/F
200   J=2/9/S
210   K=2/9/T
219   REM - COMPUTE USING APPROXIMATION FORMULAS
220   Y=ABS((1-K)*Z↑(1/3)-1+J)/SQR(K*Z↑(2/3)+J)
230   IF T<4  THEN  270
240   X=.5/(1+Y*(.196854+Y*(.115194+Y*(.000344+Y*.019527))))↑4
250   X=INT(X*10000+.5)/10000
260   GOTO  290
270   Y=Y*(1+.08*Y↑4/T↑3)
280   GOTO  240
289   REM - ADJUST IF INVERSE WAS COMPUTED
290   IF F>=1  THEN  310
300   X=1-X
310   PRINT "PERCENTILE =";1-X
320   PRINT
330   GOTO  40
340   END
```

OPTION

You may prefer to compute the tail-end value (the area of the unshaded region in the figure above). The program changes necessary are listed following the examples below.

Examples:

What is the tail-end value on an F-distribution curve when the F-value is .474 and the degrees of freedom are 1 and 18?

What is the tail-end value when the F-value is 23.7 and the degrees of freedom are 3 and 6?

```
:RUN
F-DISTRIBUTION

(TO END PROGRAM ENTER AN F-VALUE OF 0)
F-VALUE? .474
DEGREES OF FREEDOM IN NUMERATOR? 1
DEGREES OF FREEDOM IN DENOMINATOR? 18
TAIL END VALUE = .5063

F-VALUE? 23.7
DEGREES OF FREEDOM IN NUMERATOR? 3
DEGREES OF FREEDOM IN DENOMINATOR? 6
TAIL END VALUE = 1.60000000E-03

F-VALUE? 0

END PROGRAM


PROGRAM LISTING

    1    REM - OPTION 310
   10    PRINT "F-DISTRIBUTION"
    ⋮
  300    X=1-X
  310    PRINT "TAIL END VALUE =";X
  320    PRINT
  330    GOTO    40
  340    END
```

Linear Correlation Coefficient

This program computes the coefficient of correlation between two variables. A linear relationship is assumed between the variables. You must enter the coordinates of a group of data points forming the regression line.

Example:

The height of twelve men and their sons is recorded in the table below. What is the coefficient of correlation between the heights of fathers and the heights of their sons?

father	65	63	67	64	68	62	70	66	68	67	69	71
son	68	66	68	65	69	66	68	65	71	67	68	70

height in inches

```
:RUN
LINEAR CORRELATION COEFFICIENT

NUMBER OF POINTS? 12
X,Y OF POINT 1 ? 65,68
X,Y OF POINT 2 ? 63,66
X,Y OF POINT 3 ? 67,68
X,Y OF POINT 4 ? 64,65
X,Y OF POINT 5 ? 68,69
X,Y OF POINT 6 ? 62,66
X,Y OF POINT 7 ? 70,68
X,Y OF POINT 8 ? 66,65
X,Y OF POINT 9 ? 68,71
X,Y OF POINT 10 ? 67,67
X,Y OF POINT 11 ? 69,68
X,Y OF POINT 12 ? 71,70

COEFFICIENT OF CORRELATION = .7026516450773

END PROGRAM


PROGRAM LISTING

    10   PRINT "LINEAR CORRELATION COEFFICIENT"
    20   PRINT
    30   PRINT "NUMBER OF POINTS";
    40   INPUT N
    50   J=0
    60   K=0
    70   L=0
    80   M=0
    90   R=0
    99   REM - ENTER COORDINATES OF DATA POINTS
   100   FOR I=1  TO N
   110   PRINT "X,Y OF POINT";I;
   120   INPUT X,Y
   129   REM - ACCUMULATE INTERMEDIATE VALUES
```

```
130    J=J+X
140    K=K+Y
150    L=L+X↑2
160    M=M+Y↑2
170    R=R+X*Y
180    NEXT I
189    REM - CALCULATE COEFFICIENT, PRINT
190    R2=(N*R-J*K)/SQR((N*L-J↑2)*(N*M-K↑2))
200    PRINT
210    PRINT "COEFFICIENT OF CORRELATION =";R2
220    END
```

Linear Regression

This program fits a straight line to a given set of coordinates using the method of least squares. The equation of the line, coefficient of determination, coefficient of correlation and standard error of estimate are printed. Once the line has been fitted, you may predict values of *y* for given values of *x* .

Example:

The table below shows the height and weight of 11 male college students. Fit a curve to these points. How much would the average 70″ and 72″ male student weigh?

height (in.)	71	73	64	65	61	70	65	72	63	67	64
weight (lbs.)	160	183	154	168	159	180	145	210	132	168	141

```
:RUN
LINEAR REGRESSION

NUMBER OF KNOWN POINTS? 11
X,Y OF POINT 1 ? 71,160
X,Y OF POINT 2 ? 73,183
X,Y OF POINT 3 ? 64,154
X,Y OF POINT 4 ? 65,168
X,Y OF POINT 5 ? 61,159
X,Y OF POINT 6 ? 70,180
X,Y OF POINT 7 ? 65,145
X,Y OF POINT 8 ? 72,210
X,Y OF POINT 9 ? 63,132
X,Y OF POINT 10 ? 67,168
X,Y OF POINT 11 ? 64,141

F(X) =-106.7916666666 + ( 4.047222222222 * X )

COEFFICIENT OF DETERMINATION (R↑2) = .5562601669757
COEFFICIENT OF CORRELATION = .74582851043
STANDARD ERROR OF ESTIMATE = 15.41348816

INTERPOLATION: (ENTER X=0 TO END PROGRAM)
X =? 70
Y = 176.5138888889

X =? 72
Y = 184.6083333334

X =? 0

END PROGRAM
```

```
 10    PRINT "LINEAR REGRESSION"
 20    PRINT
 30    PRINT "NUMBER OF KNOWN POINTS";
 40    INPUT N
 50    J=0
 60    K=0
 70    L=0
 80    M=0
 90    R2=0
 99    REM - LOOP TO ENTER COORDINATES OF POINTS
100    FOR I=1  TO N
110    PRINT "X,Y OF POINT";I;
120    INPUT X,Y
129    REM - ACCUMULATE INTERMEDIATE SUMS
130    J=J+X
140    K=K+Y
150    L=L+X↑2
160    M=M+Y↑2
170    R2=R2+X*Y
180    NEXT I
189    REM - COMPUTE CURVE COEFFICIENT
190    B=(N*R2-K*J)/(N*L-J↑2)
200    A=(K-B*J)/N
210    PRINT
220    PRINT "F(X) =";A;"+ (";B;"* X )"
229    REM - COMPUTE REGRESSION ANALYSIS
230    J=B*(R2-J*K/N)
240    M=M-K↑2/N
250    K=M-J
260    PRINT
270    R2=J/M
280    PRINT "COEFFICIENT OF DETERMINATION (R↑2) =";R2
290    PRINT "COEFFICIENT OF CORRELATION =";SQR(R2)
300    PRINT "STANDARD ERROR OF ESTIMATE =";SQR(K/(N-2))
310    PRINT
319    REM - ESTIMATE Y-COORDINATES OF POINTS WITH ENTERED X-COORDINATES
320    PRINT "INTERPOLATION: (ENTER X=0 TO END PROGRAM)"
330    PRINT "X =";
340    INPUT X
349    REM - RESTART OR END PROGRAM?
350    IF X=0  THEN  390
360    PRINT "Y =";A+B*X
370    PRINT
380    GOTO  330
390    END
```

Multiple Linear Regression

This program finds the coefficients of a multiple variable linear equation using the method of least squares. The equation is of the following form:

$$y = c + a_1 x_1 + a_2 x_2 + \ldots a_n x_n$$

where: y = dependent variable
c = constant
$a_1, a_2 \ldots a_n$ = coefficients of independent variables $x_1, x_2, \ldots x_n$

The constant and the coefficients are printed.

You must provide the x- and y-coordinates of known data points. Once the equation has been found using the data you enter, you may predict values of the dependent variables for given values of the independent variables.

The dimension statement at line 30 limits the number of known data points the equation may contain. You can change this limit according to the following scheme:

```
30 DIM X(N+1), S(N+1), T(N+1), A(N+1,N+2)
```

where N = the number of known data points.

Example:

The table below shows the age, height and weight of eight boys. Using weight as the dependent variable, fit a curve to the data. Estimate the weight of a seven year old boy who is 51 inches tall.

age	8	9	6	10	8	9	9	7
height	48	49	44	59	55	51	55	50
weight	59	55	50	80	61	75	67	58

```
:RUN
MULTIPLE LINEAR REGRESSION

NUMBER OF KNOWN POINTS? 8
NUMBER OF INDEPENDENT VARIABLES? 2
POINT 1
   VARIABLE 1 ? 8
   VARIABLE 2 ? 48
   DEPENDENT VARIABLE? 59
POINT 2
   VARIABLE 1 ? 9
   VARIABLE 2 ? 49
   DEPENDENT VARIABLE? 55
POINT 3
   VARIABLE 1 ? 6
   VARIABLE 2 ? 44
   DEPENDENT VARIABLE? 50
```

```
POINT 4
  VARIABLE 1 ? 10
  VARIABLE 2 ? 59
  DEPENDENT VARIABLE? 80
POINT 5
  VARIABLE 1 ? 8
  VARIABLE 2 ? 55
  DEPENDENT VARIABLE? 61
POINT 6
  VARIABLE 1 ? 9
  VARIABLE 2 ? 51
  DEPENDENT VARIABLE? 75
POINT 7
  VARIABLE 1 ? 9
  VARIABLE 2 ? 55
  DEPENDENT VARIABLE? 67
POINT 8
  VARIABLE 1 ? 7
  VARIABLE 2 ? 50
  DEPENDENT VARIABLE? 58

EQUATION COEFFICIENTS:
      CONSTANT:-15.70212765959
VARIABLE( 1 ): 3.680851063828
VARIABLE( 2 ): .9432624113481

COEFFICIENT OF DETERMINATION (R↑2) = .7156973588726
COEFFICIENT OF MULTIPLE CORRELATION = .84598898271
STANDARD ERROR OF ESTIMATE = 6.4288798755

INTERPOLATION: (ENTER 0 TO END PROGRAM)
VARIABLE 1 ? 7
VARIABLE 2 ? 51
DEPENDENT VARIABLE = 58.17021276596

VARIABLE 1 ? 0

END PROGRAM


PROGRAM LISTING

   10   PRINT "MULTIPLE LINEAR REGRESSION"
   20   PRINT
   29   REM - SET ARRAY LIMITS TO X(N+1),S(N+1),T(N+1),A(N+1,N+2)
   30   DIM X(9),S(9),T(9),A(9,10)
   40   PRINT "NUMBER OF KNOWN POINTS";
   50   INPUT N
   60   PRINT "NUMBER OF INDEPENDENT VARIABLES";
   70   INPUT V
   80   X(1)=1
   90   FOR I=1  TO N
  100   PRINT "POINT";I
  110   FOR J=1  TO V
  119   REM - ENTER INDEPENDENT VARIABLES FOR EACH POINT
  120   PRINT "  VARIABLE";J;
  130   INPUT X(J+1)
```

```
140    NEXT J
149    REM - ENTER DEPENDENT VARIABLE FOR EACH POINT
150    PRINT "  DEPENDENT VARIABLE";
160    INPUT X(V+2)
169    REM - POPULATE A MATRIX TO BE USED IN CURVE FITTING
170    FOR K=1  TO V+1
180    FOR L=1  TO V+2
190    A(K,L)=A(K,L)+X(K)*X(L)
200    S(K)=A(K,V+2)
210    NEXT L
220    NEXT K
230    S(V+2)=S(V+2)+X(V+2)↑2
240    NEXT I
248    REM - STATEMENTS 250 TO 500 FIT CURVE BY SOLVING THE SYSTEM OF
249    REM - LINEAR EQUATIONS IN MATRIX A()
250    FOR I=2  TO V+1
260    T(I)=A(1,I)
270    NEXT I
280    FOR I=1  TO V+1
290    J=I
300    IF A(J,I)<>0  THEN  340
305    J=J+1
310    IF J<=V+1  THEN  300
320    PRINT "NO UNIQUE SOLUTION"
330    GOTO  810
340    FOR K=1  TO V+2
350    B=A(I,K)
360    A(I,K)=A(J,K)
370    A(J,K)=B
380    NEXT K
390    Z=1/A(I,I)
400    FOR K=1  TO V+2
410    A(I,K)=Z*A(I,K)
420    NEXT K
430    FOR J=1  TO V+1
440    IF J=I  THEN  490
450    Z=-A(J,I)
460    FOR K=1  TO V+2
470    A(J,K)=A(J,K)+Z*A(I,K)
480    NEXT K
490    NEXT J
500    NEXT I
510    PRINT
520    PRINT "EQUATION COEFFICIENTS:"
525    PRINT "       CONSTANT:";A(1,V+2)
530    FOR I=2  TO V+1
540    PRINT "VARIABLE(";I-1;"):";A(I,V+2)
550    NEXT I
560    P=0
570    FOR I=2  TO V+1
580    P=P+A(I,V+2)*(S(I)-T(I)*S(1)/N)
590    NEXT I
600    R=S(V+2)-S(1)↑2/N
610    Z=R-P
620    L=N-V-1
640    PRINT
650    I=P/R
```

```
660    PRINT "COEFFICIENT OF DETERMINATION (R↑2) =";I
670    PRINT "COEFFICIENT OF MULTIPLE CORRELATION =";SQR(I)
680    PRINT "STANDARD ERROR OF ESTIMATE ="; SQR(ABS(Z/L))
690    PRINT
699    REM - ESTIMATE DEPENDENT VARIABLE FROM ENTERED INDEPENDENT VARIAB
    LES
700    PRINT "INTERPOLATION: (ENTER 0 TO END PROGRAM)"
710    P=A(1,V+2)
720    FOR J=1  TO V
730    PRINT "VARIABLE";J;
740    INPUT X
749    REM - TEST FOR END OF PROGRAM
750    IF X=0  THEN  810
760    P=P+A(J+1,V+2)*X
770    NEXT J
780    PRINT "DEPENDENT VARIABLE =";P
790    PRINT
800    GOTO  710
810    END
```

N th Order Regression

This program finds the coefficients of an N th order equation using the method of least squares. The equation is of the following form:

$$y = c + a_1 x + a_2 x^2 + \ldots a_n x^n$$

where: y = dependent variable
c = constant
$a_1, a_2 \ldots a_n$ = coefficients of independent variables $x, x^2, \ldots x^n$, respectively

The equation coefficients, coefficient of determination, coefficient of correlation and standard error of estimate are printed.

You must provide the x - and y -coordinates for known data points. Once the equation has been computed you may predict values of y for given values of x.

The dimension statement at line 30 limits the degree of the equation. You can change this limit according to the following scheme:

$$30 \ DIM \ A(2 \cdot D + 1), \ R(D+1, D+2), \ T(D+2)$$

where D = maximum degree of equation.

Example:

The table below gives the stopping distance (reaction plus braking distance) of an automobile at various speeds. Fit an exponential curve to the data. Estimate the stopping distance at 55 m.p.h.

m.p.h.	20	30	40	50	60	70
stopping distance	54	90	138	206	292	396

```
:30 DIM A(5),R(3,4),T(4)
:RUN
NTH-ORDER REGRESSION

DEGREE OF EQUATION? 2
NUMBER OF KNOWN POINTS? 6
X,Y OF POINT 1 ? 20,54
X,Y OF POINT 2 ? 30,90
X,Y OF POINT 3 ? 40,138
X,Y OF POINT 4 ? 50,206
X,Y OF POINT 5 ? 60,292
X,Y OF POINT 6 ? 70,396

        CONSTANT = 41.771428569
 1 DEGREE COEFFICIENT =-1.095714285598
 2 DEGREE COEFFICIENT = 8.78571428E-02


COEFFICIENT OF DETERMINATION (R↑2) = .9999279597663
COEFFICIENT OF CORRELATION = .99996397923
STANDARD ERROR OF ESTIMATE = 1.4209319536
```

```
INTERPOLATION:(ENTER 0 TO END PROGRAM)
X =? 55
Y = 247.2750000003

X =? 0

END PROGRAM


PROGRAM LISTING

  10   PRINT "NTH-ORDER REGRESSION"
  20   PRINT
  29   REM - SET LIMITS ON DEGREE OF EQUATION TO A(2D+1),R(D+1,D+2),T(D+2
       (WHERE D=MAXIMUM DEGREE OF EQUATION)
  30   DIM A(13),R(7,8),T(8)
  40   PRINT "DEGREE OF EQUATION";
  50   INPUT D
  60   PRINT "NUMBER OF KNOWN POINTS";
  70   INPUT N
  80   A(1)=N
  89   REM - ENTER COORDINATES OF DATA POINTS
  90   FOR I=1  TO N
 100   PRINT "X,Y OF POINT";I;
 110   INPUT X,Y
 118   REM - LINES 120-200 POPULATE MATRICES WITH
 119   REM - A SYSTEM OF EQUATIONS
 120   FOR J=2  TO 2*D+1
 130   A(J)=A(J)+X↑(J-1)
 140   NEXT J
 150   FOR K=1  TO D+1
 160   R(K,D+2)=T(K)+Y*X↑(K-1)
 170   T(K)=T(K)+Y*X↑(K-1)
 180   NEXT K
 190   T(D+2)=T(D+2)+Y↑2
 200   NEXT I
 209   REM - LINES 210-490 SOLVE THE SYSTEM OF EQUATIONS IN THE MATRICES
 210   FOR J=1  TO D+1
 220   FOR K=1  TO D+1
 230   R(J,K)=A(J+K-1)
 240   NEXT K
 250   NEXT J
 260   FOR J=1  TO D+1
 270   K=J
 280   IF R(K,J)<>0  THEN  320
 290   K=K+1
 295   IF K<=D+1  THEN  280
 300   PRINT "NO UNIQUE SOLUTION"
 310   GOTO  790
 320   FOR I=1  TO D+2
 330   S=R(J,I)
 340   R(J,I)=R(K,I)
 350   R(K,I)=S
 360   NEXT I
 370   Z=1/R(J,J)
 380   FOR I=1  TO D+2
 390   R(J,I)=Z*R(J,I)
 400   NEXT I
```

152

```
410   FOR K=1   TO D+1
420   IF K=J   THEN   470
430   Z=-R(K,J)
440   FOR I=1   TO D+2
450   R(K,I)=R(K,I)+Z*R(J,I)
460   NEXT I
470   NEXT K
480   NEXT J
490   PRINT
495   PRINT "                CONSTANT =";R(1,D+2)
499   REM - PRINT EQUATION COEFFICIENTS.
500   FOR J=1   TO D
510   PRINT J;"DEGREE COEFFICIENT =";R(J+1,D+2)
520   NEXT J
530   PRINT
539   REM - COMPUTE REGRESSION ANALYSIS
540   P=0
550   FOR J=2   TO D+1
560   P=P+R(J,D+2)*(T(J)-A(J)*T(1)/N)
570   NEXT J
580   Q=T(D+2)-T(1)↑2/N
590   Z=Q-P
600   I=N-D-1
620   PRINT
630   J=P/Q
640   PRINT "COEFFICIENT OF DETERMINATION (R↑2) =";J
650   PRINT "COEFFICIENT OF CORRELATION =";SQR(J)
660   PRINT "STANDARD ERROR OF ESTIMATE =";SQR(Z/I)
670   PRINT
679   REM - COMPUTE Y-COORDINATE FROM ENTERED X -COORDINATE
680   PRINT "INTERPOLATION:(ENTER 0 TO END PROGRAM)"
690   P=R(1,D+2)
700   PRINT "X =";
710   INPUT X
720   IF X=0   THEN   790
730   FOR J=1   TO D
740   P=P+R(J+1,D+2)*X↑J
750   NEXT J
760   PRINT "Y =";P
770   PRINT
780   GOTO   690
790   END
```

Geometric Regression

This program fits a geometric curve to a set of coordinates using the method of least squares. The equation, coefficient of determination, coefficient of correlation and standard error of estimate are printed.

You must provide the x - and y -coordinates of known data points. Once the curve has been fitted you may predict values of y for given values of x .

Example:

The table below gives the pressures of a gas measured at various volumes in an experiment. The relationship between pressure and volume of a gas is expressed by the following formula:

$$PV^K = C$$

where: P = pressure
V = volume
C and K are constants.

This formula can be rewritten in standard geometric form:

$$P = CV^{-K}$$

Note the exponent is negative, which accounts for the negative exponents the program calculates.

Fit a geometric curve to the data and estimate the pressure of 90 cubic inches of the gas.

volume	56.1	60.7	73.2	88.3	120.1	187.5
pressure	57.0	51.0	39.2	30.2	19.6	10.5

```
:RUN
GEOMETRIC REGRESSION

NUMBER OF KNOWN POINTS? 6
X,Y OF POINT 1 ? 56.1,57.0
X,Y OF POINT 2 ? 60.7,51.0
X,Y OF POINT 3 ? 73.2,39.2
X,Y OF POINT 4 ? 88.3,30.2
X,Y OF POINT 5 ? 120.1,19.6
X,Y OF POINT 6 ? 187.5,10.5

F(X) = 16103.68991715 * X↑-1.401550582441

COEFFICIENT OF DETERMINATION (R↑2) = .9999988312731
COEFFICIENT OF CORRELATION = .99999941564
STANDARD ERROR OF ESTIMATE = 7.73614568E-04

INTERPOLATION: (ENTER X=0 TO END PROGRAM)
X =? 90
Y = 29.37349825098

X =? 0

END PROGRAM
```

PROGRAM LISTING

```
10    PRINT "GEOMETRIC REGRESSION"
20    PRINT
30    PRINT "NUMBER OF KNOWN POINTS";
40    INPUT N
50    J=0
60    K=0
70    L=0
80    M=0
90    R2=0
99    REM - ENTER COORDINATES OF DATA POINTS
100   FOR I=1  TO N
110   PRINT "X,Y OF POINT";I;
120   INPUT X,Y
129   REM - ACCUMULATE INTERMEDIATE VALUES
130   Y=LOG(Y)
140   X=LOG(X)
150   J=J+X
160   K=K+Y
170   L=L+X↑2
180   M=M+Y↑2
190   R2=R2+X*Y
200   NEXT I
209   REM - CALCULATE AND PRINT COEFFICIENTS OF EQUATION
210   B=(N*R2-K*J)/(N*L-J↑2)
220   A=(K-B*J)/N
230   PRINT
240   PRINT "F(X) =";EXP(A);"* X↑";B
249   REM - CALCULATE REGRESSION ANALYSIS
250   J=B*(R2-J*K/N)
260   M=M-K↑2/N
270   K=M-J
280   PRINT
290   R2=J/M
300   PRINT "COEFFICIENT OF DETERMINATION (R↑2) =";R2
310   PRINT "COEFFICIENT OF CORRELATION =";SQR(R2)
320   PRINT "STANDARD ERROR OF ESTIMATE =";SQR(K/(N-2))
330   PRINT
339   REM - ESTIMATE Y-COORDINATE FROM ENTERED X-COORDINATE
340   PRINT "INTERPOLATION: (ENTER X=0 TO END PROGRAM)"
350   PRINT "X =";
360   INPUT X
370   IF X=0  THEN  410
380   PRINT "Y =";EXP(A)*X↑B
390   PRINT
400   GOTO  350
410   END
```

Exponential Regression

This program finds the coefficients of an equation for an exponential curve. The equation is in the following form:

$$f(x) = ae^{bx}$$

where *a* and *b* are the calculated coefficients.

The equation coefficients, coefficient of determination, coefficient of correlation and standard error of estimate are printed.

You must provide the *x*- and *y*-coordinates for known data points. Once the curve has been fitted you may predict values of *y* for given values of *x*.

Example:

The table below shows the number of bacteria present in a culture at various points in time. Fit an exponential curve to the data and estimate the number of bacteria after 7 hours.

number of hours	0	1	2	3	4	5	6
number of bacteria	25	38	58	89	135	206	315

```
:RUN
EXPONENTIAL REGRESSION

NUMBER OF KNOWN POINTS? 7
X,Y OF POINT 1 ? 0,25
X,Y OF POINT 2 ? 1,38
X,Y OF POINT 3 ? 2,58
X,Y OF POINT 4 ? 3,89
X,Y OF POINT 5 ? 4,135
X,Y OF POINT 6 ? 5,206
X,Y OF POINT 7 ? 6,315

A = 24.96166337346
B = .4223750795699

COEFFICIENT OF DETERMINATION (R↑2) = .9999935513734
COEFFICIENT OF CORRELATION = .99999677568
STANDARD ERROR OF ESTIMATE = 2.53820862E-03

INTERPOLATION: (ENTER X=0 TO END PROGRAM)
X =? 7
Y = 480.0867130787

X =? 0

END PROGRAM
```

PROGRAM LISTING

```
10    PRINT "EXPONENTIAL REGRESSION"
20    PRINT
30    PRINT "NUMBER OF KNOWN POINTS";
40    INPUT N
50    J=0
60    K=0
70    L=0
80    M=0
90    R2=0
99    REM - ENTER COORDINATES OF DATA POINTS
100   FOR I=1  TO N
110   PRINT "X,Y OF POINT";T;
120   INPUT X,Y
129   REM - ACCUMULATE INTERMEDIATE VALUES
130   Y=LOG(Y)
140   J=J+X
150   K=K+Y
160   L=L+X↑2
170   M=M+Y↑2
180   R2=R2+X*Y
190   NEXT I
199   REM - CALCULATE AND PRINT COEFFICIENTS OF EQUATION
200   B=(N*R2-K*J)/(N*L-J↑2)
210   A=(K-B*J)/N
220   PRINT
230   PRINT "A =";EXP(A)
240   PRINT "B =";B
249   REM - CALCULATE REGRESSION TABLE VALUES
250   J=B*(R2-J*K/N)
260   M=M-K↑2/N
270   K=M-J
280   PRINT
290   R2=J/M
300   PRINT "COEFFICIENT OF DETERMINATION (R↑2) =";R2
310   PRINT "COEFFICIENT OF CORRELATION =";SQR(R2)
320   PRINT "STANDARD ERROR OF ESTIMATE =";SQR(K/(N-2))
330   PRINT
339   REM - ESTIMATE Y-VALUE FROM ENTERED X-VALUE
340   PRINT "INTERPOLATION: (ENTER X=0 TO END PROGRAM)"
350   PRINT "X =";
360   INPUT X
370   IF X=0  THEN  410
380   PRINT "Y =";EXP(A)*EXP(B*X)
390   PRINT
400   GOTO  350
410   END
```

System Reliability

This program calculates the reliability of an operating system that is subject to wearout and chance failure. You must enter the system's operating time and the wearout time and failure rate of each component.

Example:

Compute the reliability of a computer system operating for 1000 hours with the components shown in the list below.

	wearout (hrs.)	failure
CPU	15,000	.00020
terminal	3,000	.00010
disk	3,000	.00015
printer	1,500	.00015

```
:RUN
SYSTEM RELIABILITY

(TO END PROGRAM ENTER 0)
OPERATING TIME IN HOURS? 1000
NUMBER OF COMPONENTS? 4
COMPONENT 1
   AVERAGE WEAROUT TIME? 15000
   AVERAGE FAILURE RATE? .0002
COMPONENT 2
   AVERAGE WEAROUT TIME? 3000
   AVERAGE FAILURE RATE? .0001
COMPONENT 3
   AVERAGE WEAROUT TIME? 3000
   AVERAGE FAILURE RATE? .00015
COMPONENT 4
   AVERAGE WEAROUT TIME? 1500
   AVERAGE FAILURE RATE? .00015

SYSTEM RELIABILITY = .1353352832367

OPERATING TIME IN HOURS? 0

END PROGRAM
```

PROGRAM LISTING

```
10   PRINT "SYSTEM RELIABILITY"
20   PRINT
30   PRINT "(TO END PROGRAM ENTER 0)"
40   PRINT "OPERATING TIME IN HOURS";
50   INPUT T
```

```
59    REM - TEST FOR END OF PROGRAM
60    IF T=0   THEN  230
70    PRINT "NUMBER OF COMPONENTS";
80    INPUT N
90    Z=0
99    REM - ENTER DATA FOR EACH COMPONENT
100   FOR I=1   TO N
110   PRINT "COMPONENT";I
120   PRINT "  AVERAGE WEAROUT TIME";
130   INPUT W
140   PRINT "  AVERAGE FAILURE RATE";
150   INPUT F
159   REM - INCLUDE EACH COMPONENT IN RELIABILITY
160   Z=Z+1/W+F
170   NEXT I
180   PRINT
189   REM - CALCULATE RELIABILITY, PRINT
190   Z=EXP(-Z*T)
200   PRINT "SYSTEM RELIABILITY =";Z
210   PRINT
219   REM - RESTART PROGRAM
220   GOTO    40
230   END
```

Average Growth Rate, Future Projections

This program calculates the average growth rate of a company, then projects figures for future years. The growth rate and projections could be computed for any aspect of a company, such as sales, earnings, number of employees, or patronage. You must provide established figures for a past series of years.

The dimension statement at line 30 limits the number of past figures you may enter. Any need to alter this limit should be done in the following manner:

$$30 \text{ DIM } S(N)$$

where N = the number of years for which figures are known.

Example:

The borrowing records for Claremount County Library are tabulated in the graph below. What is its average growth rate? How many books can it expect to lend in its tenth and twentieth years of service?

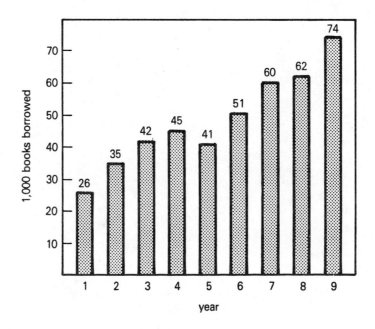

year

```
:30 DIM S(9)
:RUN
AVERAGE GROWTH RATE, FUTURE PROJECTIONS

NUMBER OF YEARS FIGURES ESTABLISHED? 9
FIGURE: YEAR 1 ? 26
        YEAR 2 ? 35
        YEAR 3 ? 42
        YEAR 4 ? 45
        YEAR 5 ? 41
        YEAR 6 ? 51
        YEAR 7 ? 60
        YEAR 8 ? 62
        YEAR 9 ? 74
AVERAGE GROWTH RATE = 11.88 %
```

```
(ENTER 0 TO END PROGRAM)
PROJECTED SALES FOR YEAR? 10
                                = 81.29
PROJECTED SALES FOR YEAR? 20
                                = 249.88
PROJECTED SALES FOR YEAR? 0

END PROGRAM


PROGRAM LISTING

   10    PRINT "AVERAGE GROWTH RATE, FUTURE PROJECTIONS"
   20    PRINT
   29    REM - SET ARRAY S TO NUMBER OF YEARS PAST FIGURES KNOWN
   30    DIM S(20)
   39    REM - STATEMENTS 40 TO 120 REQUEST USER INPUT
   40    PRINT "NUMBER OF YEARS FIGURES ESTABLISHED";
   50    INPUT N
   60    FOR I=1  TO N
   70    IF I>1  THEN  100
   80    PRINT "FIGURE: YEAR";I;
   90    GOTO  110
  100    PRINT "          YEAR";I;
  110    INPUT S(I)
  120    NEXT I
  129    REM - INITIALIZE VARIABLES FOR FIRST YEAR
  130    T=LOG(S(1))
  140    V=0
  149    REM - LOOP FOR REMAINING YEARS OF HISTORY
  150    FOR I=2  TO N
  160    L=LOG(S(I))
  170    T=T+L
  180    V=V+(I-1)*L
  190    NEXT I
  199    REM - CALCULATE AVERAGE GROWTH RATE
  200    A=6*(2*V/(N-1)-T)/(N)/(N+1)
  210    G=EXP(A)-1
  219    REM - ROUND OFF, PRINT
  220    PRINT "AVERAGE GROWTH RATE =";INT.(G*10000+.5)/100;"%"
  230    PRINT
  239    REM - CALCULATE AVERAGE ANNUAL GROWTH FACTOR
  240    S=EXP(T/N-A*(N-1)/2)
  250    PRINT "(ENTER 0 TO END PROGRAM)"
  259    REM - INPUT YEAR NUMBER
  260    PRINT "PROJECTED SALES FOR YEAR";
  270    INPUT Y1
  279    REM - TEST FOR END OF PROGRAM
  280    IF Y1=0  THEN  320
  289    REM - CALCULATE PROJECTED SALES FIGURE
  290    S1=S*(1+G)^(Y1-1)
  299    REM - ROUND OFF, PRINT
  300    PRINT "                                =";INT(S1*100+.5)/100
  309    REM - RETURN FOR MORE DATA
  310    GOTO  260
  320    END
```

Federal Withholding Taxes

This program calculates the amount of federal income and FICA taxes withheld from one's earnings. You must provide employee information as to marital status, the number of exemptions claimed, the amount of taxable pay, and year-to-date taxable pay.

The number of pay periods per year is established at line 80. If your pay period is other than monthly, you must alter this statement to set *N* equal to the number of pay periods per year.

There is a considerable amount of tax information which may change from year to year. The values listed in the data tables at lines 30 and 40 are among those that may need periodic revision. The annual values for single and married persons should be compared each year with those listed in Table 7 of the current IRS Circular E.

The annual FICA rate, the FICA cutoff amount and the annual amount of withholding allowance may also need revision. The values established at lines 50, 60 and 70 should also be compared to those listed in the current IRS circular.

Annual rates and cutoffs are used irrespective of your actual pay period frequency. The program automatically adjusts them to match your pay period.

Examples:

Judy earns $900.00 per month. The payroll clerk is figuring her March paycheck. Judy is single and claims only herself as a dependent. What amounts are withheld from her paycheck?

Dr. Berger has earned $1,408.75 this month. So far this year he has grossed $20,188.72. He is married and claims four dependents. What amounts will be withheld this month for the federal government?

```
:RUN
FEDERAL WITHHOLDING TAXES


MARITAL STATUS (1=SINGLE, 2=MARRIED)? 1
WITHHOLDING TAX EXEMPTIONS? 1
TAXABLE PAY? 900
YTD TAXABLE PAY? 1800
TAXABLE = $ 900
INCOME TAX = $ 128.5
FICA = $ 55.17

MORE DATA (1=YES, 0=NO)? 1

MARITAL STATUS (1=SINGLE, 2=MARRIED)? 2
WITHHOLDING TAX EXEMPTIONS? 4
TAXABLE PAY? 1408.75
YTD TAXABLE PAY? 23750.03
TAXABLE = $ 1408.75
INCOME TAX = $ 152.09
FICA = $ 0

MORE DATA (1=YES, 0=NO)? 0
```

```
10    PRINT "FEDERAL WITHHOLDING TAXES"
20    PRINT
27    REM - THE FOLLOWING DATA CONTAINS THE 1980 TAX TABLES FROM IRS
28    REM - CIRCULAR E, PERCENTAGE METHOD, TABLE 7 (ANNUAL PAYROLL)
29    REM - FOR SINGLE PERSONS
30    DATA 15,1420,18,3300,21,6800,26,10200,30,14200,34,17200,39,22500
39    REM - FOR MARRIED PERSONS
40    DATA 15,2400,18,6600,21,10900,24,15000,28,19200,32,23600,37,28900
49    REM - F1=FICA RATE AS DECIMAL
50    F1=.0613
59    REM - F2=FICA CUTOFF AMOUNT
60    F2=25900
69    REM - W1=AMOUNT OF WITHHOLDING ALLOWANCE (ANNUAL PAYROLL)
70    W1=1000
79    REM - N=NUMBER OF PAY PERIODS PER YEAR
80    N=12
89    REM - LOAD THE TAX TABLE ARRAYS FROM DATA TABLES
90    DIM F1(28)
100   FOR I=1  TO 28
110   READ F1(I)
120   NEXT I
130   PRINT
139   REM - STATEMENTS 140 TO 210 REQUEST PERTINENT EMPLOYEE DATA
140   PRINT "MARITAL STATUS (1=SINGLE, 2=MARRIED)";
150   INPUT S
160   PRINT "WITHHOLDING TAX EXEMPTIONS";
170   INPUT W
180   PRINT "TAXABLE PAY";
190   INPUT P
199   REM - Y=TOTAL TAXABLE PAY THIS YEAR, EXCLUDING CURRENT PAYCHECK
200   PRINT "YTD TAXABLE PAY";
210   INPUT Y
219   REM - ANNUALIZE CURRENT TAXABLE PAY, ADJUST FOR EXEMPTIONS
220   G=P*N-W1*W
230   T1=0
239   REM - CALCULATE INCOME TAX
240   FOR I=2  TO 7
250   X=2*I+14*(S-1)-1
260   IF G<=F1(X-1)  THEN  330
270   IF G>F1(X+1)  THEN  300
280   T1=T1+(G-F1(X-1))*F1(X-2)/100
290   GOTO  330
300   T1=T1+(F1(X+1)-F1(X-1))*F1(X-2)/100
310   NEXT I
320   T1=T1+(G-F1(X+1))*F1(X)/100
329   REM - ROUND OFF TO NEAREST CENT
330   T1=INT((T1/N)*100+.5)/100
340   T2=0
349   REM - CALCULATE FICA
350   IF Y>F2  THEN  400
360   IF Y+P>F2  THEN  390
370   T2=INT((P*F1)*100+.5)/100
380   GOTO  400
389   REM - ROUND OFF TO NEAREST CENT
390   T2=INT(((F2-Y)*F1)*100+.5)/100
```

```
399    REM - PRINT RESULTS
400    PRINT "TAXABLE = $";P
410    PRINT "INCOME TAX = $";T1
420    PRINT "FICA = $";T2
430    PRINT
439    REM - RESTART OR END PROGRAM?
440    PRINT "MORE DATA (1=YES, 0=NO)";
450    INPUT S
460    IF S=1   THEN   130
470    END
```

Tax Depreciation Schedule

This program tabulates annual depreciation amounts. You can use the sum of digits method or any declining balance percentage method. You must know the purchase price (initial value), salvage value at the end of the depreciable life, and the life of the item being depreciated. If you are doing declining balance depreciation, you must also know the percentage method.

Examples:

The Miracle Corporation put a new roof on their office building for $27,000.00. They expect to replace it in nine years. What would the annual depreciation amounts be using the sum of digits?

Heavenly Bank built a new home office building for $1.2 million. Run a tax depreciation schedule on the building using 150% declining balance method with a 30 year life. Assume a salvage value of $250,000. You will notice that the depreciation falls below straight line ($31,666.67) per year) at year nine.

```
:RUN
TAX DEPRECIATION SCHEDULE

PURCHASE PRICE? 27000
SALVAGE VALUE? 0
LIFE IN YEARS? 9
ENTER 1 FOR SUM OF DIGITS, 2 FOR DECLINING BALANCE? 1


        SUM OF DIGITS TAX DEPRECIATION
              PRICE $ 27000
          SALVAGE VALUE $ 0
        NET DEPRECIATED $ 27000
              LIFE 9 YEARS

YEAR              DEPRECIATION      BALANCE
1                 5400              21600
2                 4800              16800
3                 4200              12600
4                 3600              9000
5                 3000              6000
6                 2400              3600
7                 1800              1800
8                 1200              600
9                 600               0

MORE DATA?(1=YES,0=NO)? 1

PURCHASE PRICE? 1200000
SALVAGE VALUE? 250000
LIFE IN YEARS? 30
ENTER 1 FOR SUM OF DIGITS, 2 FOR DECLINING BALANCE? 2
METHOD IN %? 150
```

```
        DECLINING BALANCE TAX DEPRECIATION
              PRICE $ 1200000
          SALVAGE VALUE $ 250000
        NET DEPRECIATED $ 950000
              LIFE 30 YEARS
              METHOD   150 %
```

YEAR	DEPRECIATION	BALANCE
1	47500	902500
2	45125	857375
3	42868.75	814506.25
4	40725.31	773780.94
5	38689.05	735091.89
6	36754.59	698337.3
7	34916.87	663420.43
8	33171.02	630249.41
9	31512.47	598736.94
10	29936.85	568800.09
11	28440	540360.09
12	27018	513342.09
13	25667.1	487674.99
14	24383.75	463291.24
15	23164.56	440126.68
16	22006.33	418120.35
17	20906.02	397214.33
18	19860.72	377353.61
19	18867.68	358485.93
20	17924.3	340561.63
21	17028.08	323533.55
22	16176.68	307356.87
23	15367.84	291989.03
24	14599.45	277389.58
25	13869.48	263520.1
26	13176.01	250344.09
27	12517.2	237826.89
28	11891.34	225935.55
29	11296.78	214638.77
30	10731.94	203906.83

```
MORE DATA?(1=YES,0=NO)? 0

END PROGRAM


PROGRAM LISTING

    10   PRINT "TAX DEPRECIATION SCHEDULE"
    20   PRINT
    29   REM - ENTER INITIAL VALUE AND ROUND OFF TO NEAREST CENT
    30   PRINT "PURCHASE PRICE";
    40   INPUT V
    50   V=INT(V*100+.5)/100
    59   REM - ENTER END VALUE AND ROUND OFF TO NEAREST CENT
    60   PRINT "SALVAGE VALUE";
    70   INPUT S
    80   S=INT(S*100+.5)/100
    89   REM - COMPUTE AMOUNT TO DEPRECIATE
```

```
90     D=V-S
99     REM - ENTER LENGTH OF DEPRECIATION
100    PRINT "LIFE IN YEARS";
110    INPUT Y
119    REM - CHOOSE DEPRECIATION METHOD
120    PRINT "ENTER 1 FOR SUM OF DIGITS, 2 FOR DECLINING BALANCE";
130    INPUT X
140    IF X=2   THEN   450
150    IF X<>1   THEN   120
158    REM - BY SUM OF DIGITS METHOD
159    REM - R1 IS THE CUMULATIVE AMOUNT DEPRECIATED
160    R1=0
169    REM - N IS THE PRINTED LINE COUNTER
170    N=66
180    PRINT
190    PRINT
200    FOR I=1   TO Y
209    REM - TEST FOR FULL PAGE
210    IF N<55   THEN   330
219    REM - FULL PAGE; SPACE TO TOP OF NEXT PAGE AND PRINT HEADINGS
220    FOR I1=N   TO 66
230    PRINT
240    NEXT I1
250    N=7
260    PRINT "        SUM OF DIGITS TAX DEPRECIATION"
270    PRINT "                    PRICE $";V
280    PRINT "            SALVAGE VALUE $";S
290    PRINT "          NET DEPRECIATED $";V-S
300    PRINT "                     LIFE";Y;"YEARS"
310    PRINT
320    PRINT "YEAR","DEPRECIATION","BALANCE"
329    REM - COMPUTE DEPRECIATION AND ROUND OFF TO NEAREST CENT
330    R=2*D*(Y-I+1)/((Y+1)*Y)
340    R=INT(R*100+.5)/100
349    REM - ACCUMULATE DEPRECIATION
350    R1=R1+R
359    REM - COMPUTE BALANCE TO DEPRECIATE
360    B=D-R1
369    REM - TEST FOR COMPLETE DEPRECIATION
370    IF B>=0   THEN   410
380    R1=R1+B
390    R=R+B
400    B=0
410    PRINT I,R,B
420    N=N+1
430    NEXT I
440    GOTO   700
448    REM - BY DECLINING BALANCE METHOD
449    REM - ENTER DECLINING BALANCE PERCENT
450    PRINT "METHOD IN %";
460    INPUT M
469    REM - CONVERT PERCENT TO DECIMAL
470    M=M/100
479    REM - N   COUNTS THE LINES PRINTED ON EACH PAGE
480    N=66
489    REM - R IS THE AMOUNT LEFT TO DEPRECIATE
490    R=D
```

```
500     PRINT
510     FOR I=1   TO Y
519     REM - TEST FOR A FULL PRINTED PAGE
520     IF N<55   THEN   650
529     REM - FULL PAGE; SPACE TO TOP OF NEXT PAGE AND PRINT HEADINGS
530     FOR I1=N   TO 66
540     PRINT
550     NEXT I1
560     N=8
570     PRINT "       DECLINING BALANCE TAX DEPRECIATION"
580     PRINT "             PRICE $";V
590     PRINT "          SALVAGE VALUE $";S
600     PRINT "        NET DEPRECIATED $";D
610     PRINT "             LIFE";Y;"YEARS"
620     PRINT "             METHOD ";M*100;"%"
630     PRINT
640     PRINT "YEAR","DEPRECIATION","BALANCE"
649     REM - COMPUTE DEPRECIATION AND ROUND OFF TO THE NEAREST CENT
650     R1=INT((R*M/Y)*100+.5)/100
659     REM - ACCUMULATE REMAINING BALANCE
660     R=R-R1
670     PRINT I,R1,R
680     N=N+1
690     NEXT I
700     PRINT
709     REM - RESTART OR END PROGRAM?
710     PRINT "MORE DATA?(1=YES,0=NO)";
720     INPUT X
730     IF X=1   THEN   20
740     END
```

Check Writer

This program prints a check. You must provide the date, amount and payee of the check. The program translates the date and amount to words and prints providing spacing within the check.

You should regard the program listed below as a sample of a check-writing program. Very few checks will conform exactly to the spacing provided in this program. The method of translating words from numbers is generally applicable. Spacing should be altered to conform to your own check format.

When the program asks the question READY TO PRINT CHECK? it is prompting you to insert a blank check in your printing device. The check should be set one line above the line on which the date is to be printed.

Once the check is set up, key RETURN (no other entry is required) and the check will be printed.

Example:

Among the checks that Miracle Corporation must write are one to Osborne & Associates for $4975.89 and one to Freida Alexander for $103.75. Print the checks using the computer.

```
:RUN
CHECK WRITER

DATE (MMDDYY)? 30877
--(TO END PROGRAM ENTER 'END')--
FIRST NAME OF PAYEE? OSBORNE &
LAST NAME OF PAYEE? ASSOCIATES
AMOUNT OF CHECK? 4975.89
READY TO PRINT CHECK?
```

HEAVENLY BANK	NO. 328
EMERYVILLE OFFICE	
4120 ASHBY AVENUE	MARCH 8 19 77
EMERYVILLE, CA 94601	$ 4975.89
	AMOUNT $ 4975.89

PAY TO THE ORDER OF   OSBORNE & ASSOCIATES

FOUR THOUSAND NINE HUNDRED SEVENTY-FIVE DOLLARS AND 89 CENTS

MIRACLE CORPORATION
1111 COUNTRY ROAD
COUNTRYVILLE, CA 94132

1328252158

FIRST NAME OF PAYEE? FREIDA
LAST NAME OF PAYEE? ALEXANDER
AMOUNT OF CHECK? 103.75
READY TO PRINT CHECK?

HEAVENLY BANK   NO. 382

EMERYVILLE OFFICE
4120 ASHBY AVENUE   MARCH 8   19 77
EMERYVILLE, CA 94601 $ 103.75
                                            AMOUNT $ 103.75

PAY TO THE ORDER OF   FREIDA ALEXANDER

ONE HUNDRED THREE DOLLARS AND 75 CENTS

MIRACLE CORPORATION

1111 COUNTRY ROAD
COUNTRYVILLE, CA 94132

1328252158

FIRST NAME OF PAYEE? END

END PROGRAM

PROGRAM LISTING

```
  10   PRINT "CHECK WRITER"
  20   PRINT
  30   DATA "ONE","TWO","THREE","FOUR","FIVE","SIX","SEVEN","EIGHT","NINE"
  40   DATA "TEN","ELEVEN","TWELVE","THIRTEEN","FOURTEEN","FIFTEEN","SIXTEE
     N"
  50   DATA "SEVENTEEN","EIGHTEEN","NINETEEN","TWENTY","THIRTY","FORTY"
  60   DATA "FIFTY","SIXTY","SEVENTY","EIGHTY","NINETY"
  70   DATA "JANUARY","FEBRUARY","MARCH","APRIL","MAY","JUNE","JULY"
  80   DATA "AUGUST","SEPTEMBER","OCTOBER","NOVEMBER","DECEMBER"
  89   REM - ENTER DATE WITHOUT COMMAS; DAY AND YEAR MUST CONTAIN TWO DIGIT
     S
  90   PRINT "DATE (MMDDYY)";
 100   INPUT D
 110   PRINT "--(TO END PROGRAM ENTER 'END')--"
 120   PRINT "FIRST NAME OF PAYEE";
 130   INPUT F$
 139   REM - END PROGRAM?
 140   IF F$="END"  THEN  790
 150   PRINT "LAST NAME OF PAYEE";
 160   INPUT L$
 170   PRINT "AMOUNT OF CHECK";
 180   INPUT A
 189   REM - INSERT BLANK CHECK IN PRINTING DEVICE, KEY RETURN WHEN READY
 190   PRINT "READY TO PRINT CHECK";
 200   INPUT X
 209   REM - BREAK ENTERED DATE NUMBER INTO MONTH, DAY, YEAR FIGURES
 210   D1=INT(D/10000)
```

```
220   D2=INT((D-D1*10000)/100)
230   D3=INT(D-(D1*100+D2)*100)
239   REM - GO TO CORRECT MONTH IN DATA TABLE
240   RESTORE 27+D1
250   READ X0$
259   REM - PRINT DATE
260   PRINT ,,,X0$;D2;"   ";D3
269   REM - PRINT AMOUNT TWICE; FIRST TIME FOR SHADED BOX
270   PRINT ,,,"$";A
280   PRINT ,,," ";A
290   PRINT
300   PRINT ,F$;" ";L$
310   PRINT
319   REM - AMOUNT OF CHECK LEGITIMATE?
320   IF A<=0  THEN  770
330   A1=A
339   REM - AMOUNT IN THE THOUSANDS?
340   N1=INT(A1/1E3)
349   REM - CAN'T PRINT FOR AMOUNT OVER $99999.99
350   IF N1>99 THEN  770
360   IF N1=0  THEN  390
370   GOSUB  640
380   PRINT "THOUSAND ";
390   A1=A1-N1*1E3
399   REM - AMOUNT IN THE HUNDREDS?
400   N1=INT(A1/100)
410   IF N1=0  THEN  440
420   GOSUB  640
430   PRINT "HUNDRED ";
440   A1=A1-N1*100
449   REM - AMOUNT IN THE ONES OR TENS?
450   N1=INT(A1)
460   IF N1>0  THEN  490
470   IF A>=1  THEN  500
480   GOTO  510
490   GOSUB  640
500   PRINT "DOLLARS ";
510   A1=A1-N1
519   REM - ANY CENTS?
520   IF A1<.01  THEN  600
529   REM - IF AMOUNT IS CENTS ONLY DON'T PRINT 'AND'
530   IF A<1  THEN  550
540   PRINT "AND";
550   A1=A1*100
559   REM - CENTS ARE PRINTED IN NUMERIC FORM
560   PRINT A1;"CENTS"
569   REM - SPACE OFF OF CHECK
570   PRINT
580   PRINT
590   PRINT
600   PRINT
610   PRINT
620   PRINT
629   REM - RESTART PROGRAM
630   GOTO  120
639   REM - SUBROUTINE TO GET WORDS FOR. NUMBERS
640   IF N1<21  THEN  730
```

```
650    RESTORE (N1-20)/10+20
660    READ X0$
670    PRINT X0$;
680    A3=N1-INT(N1/10)*10
690    IF A3=0  THEN  760
700    PRINT "-";
710    RESTORE A3
720    GOTO  740
730    RESTORE N1
740    READ X0$
750    PRINT X0$;" ";
759    REM - END OF SUBROUTINE
760    RETURN
770    PRINT ,"*****VOID*****"
780    GOTO  570
790    END
```

Recipe Cost

This program calculates the cost and the cost per serving of a single recipe. For each ingredient you must provide the purchase price, the amount purchased, the amount used in the recipe, and the number of recipe units per purchase unit.

Example:

Listed below is a recipe for strawberry shortcake. Calculate the cost of the recipe and the cost per serving. What would the cost per serving be if one cake serves 12? The conversion factors and price per ingredient are supplied.

Strawberry Shortcake — 8 servings

3 c. flour	2.5 c./lb.	$1.59	5 lb.
3¼ tsp. baking powder	15 tsp./oz.	.43	4 oz.
¼ c. sugar	2 c./lb.	1.24	5 lb.
1¼ tsp. salt	6 tsp./oz.	.29	1 lb.
½ c. butter	2 c./lb.	1.49	1 lb.
1 egg	12/doz.	.75	1 doz.
⅔ c. milk	4 c./qt.	.40	1 qt.
3 pts strawberries	——	.49	1 pt.
½ pt. whipping cream	——	.59	½ pt.

```
:RUN
RECIPE COST

NUMBER OF INGREDIENTS? 9
INGREDIENT 1 :
   COST FOR BULK UNIT IN STORE? 1.59
   NUMBER OF UNITS IN BULK? 5
   NUMBER OF RECIPE UNITS PER BULK UNIT? 2.5
   NUMBER OF RECIPE UNITS CALLED FOR? 3
INGREDIENT 2 :
   COST FOR BULK UNIT IN STORE? .43
   NUMBER OF UNITS IN BULK? 4
   NUMBER OF RECIPE UNITS PER BULK UNIT? 15
   NUMBER OF RECIPE UNITS CALLED FOR? 3.25
INGREDIENT 3 :
   COST FOR BULK UNIT IN STORE? 1.24
   NUMBER OF UNITS IN BULK? 5
   NUMBER OF RECIPE UNITS PER BULK UNIT? 2
   NUMBER OF RECIPE UNITS CALLED FOR? .25
INGREDIENT 4 :
   COST FOR BULK UNIT IN STORE? .29
   NUMBER OF UNITS IN BULK? 1
   NUMBER OF RECIPE UNITS PER BULK UNIT? 96
   NUMBER OF RECIPE UNITS CALLED FOR? 1.25
INGREDIENT 5 :
   COST FOR BULK UNIT IN STORE? 1.49
   NUMBER OF UNITS IN BULK? 1
   NUMBER OF RECIPE UNITS PER BULK UNIT? 2
   NUMBER OF RECIPE UNITS CALLED FOR? .5
```

```
INGREDIENT 6 :
  COST FOR BULK UNIT IN STORE? .75
  NUMBER OF UNITS IN BULK? 1
  NUMBER OF RECIPE UNITS PER BULK UNIT? 12
  NUMBER OF RECIPE UNITS CALLED FOR? 1
INGREDIENT 7 :
  COST FOR BULK UNIT IN STORE? .40
  NUMBER OF UNITS IN BULK? 1
  NUMBER OF RECIPE UNITS PER BULK UNIT? 4
  NUMBER OF RECIPE UNITS CALLED FOR? .6666667
INGREDIENT 8 :
  COST FOR BULK UNIT IN STORE? .49
  NUMBER OF UNITS IN BULK? 1
  NUMBER OF RECIPE UNITS PER BULK UNIT? 1
  NUMBER OF RECIPE UNITS CALLED FOR? 3
INGREDIENT 9 :
  COST FOR BULK UNIT IN STORE? .59
  NUMBER OF UNITS IN BULK? 1
  NUMBER OF RECIPE UNITS PER BULK UNIT? 1
  NUMBER OF RECIPE UNITS CALLED FOR? 1
NUMBER OF SERVINGS? 8

TOTAL COST FOR 1 RECIPE = $ 3
COST PER SERVING = $ .38

CHANGE NUMBER OF SERVINGS (1=YES,0=NO)? 1
NUMBER OF SERVINGS? 12

TOTAL COST FOR 1 RECIPE = $ 3
COST PER SERVING = $ .25

CHANGE NUMBER OF SERVINGS (1=YES,0=NO)? 0

END PROGRAM
```

PROGRAM LISTING

```
  10   PRINT "RECIPE COST"
  20   PRINT
  29   REM - STATEMENTS 30 TO 180 REQUEST USER INPUT
  30   PRINT "NUMBER OF INGREDIENTS";
  40   INPUT N
  49   REM - LOOP TO REQUEST DATA FOR EACH INGREDIENT
  50   FOR I=1  TO N
  60   PRINT "INGREDIENT";I;":"
  70   PRINT "  COST FOR BULK UNIT IN STORE";
  80   INPUT C
  90   PRINT "  NUMBER OF UNITS IN BULK";
 100   INPUT U
 110   PRINT "  NUMBER OF RECIPE UNITS PER BULK UNIT";
 120   INPUT F
 130   PRINT "  NUMBER OF RECIPE UNITS CALLED FOR";
 140   INPUT R
 149   REM - SUM COST OF EACH INGREDIENT PER AMOUNT USED
 150   P=P+C/U/F*R
 160   NEXT I
```

```
170   PRINT "NUMBER OF SERVINGS";
180   INPUT S
190   PRINT
199   REM - ROUND OFF COSTS TO NEAREST CENT, PRINT RESULTS
200   PRINT "TOTAL COST FOR 1 RECIPE = $";INT(P*100+.5)/100
210   PRINT "COST PER SERVING = $";INT(P/S*100+.5)/100
220   PRINT
229   REM - CALCULATE ALTERNATIVE PRICE PER SERVING?
230   PRINT "CHANGE NUMBER OF SERVINGS (1=YES,0=NO)";
240   INPUT N
250   IF N=1  THEN  170
260   END
```

OPTION

As you become familiar with the operation of this program you may wish to shorten it by entering the information required for each ingredient on one line. The program changes necessary are listed following the example below.

Example:

Calculate the cost per serving of Strawberry Shortcake in the previous example when it is served without cream.

```
:RUN
RECIPE COST

NUMBER OF INGREDIENTS? 8
INGREDIENT 1 ? 1.59,5,2.5,3
INGREDIENT 2 ? .43,4,15,3.25
INGREDIENT 3 ? 1.24,5,2,.25
INGREDIENT 4 ? .29,1,96,1.25
INGREDIENT 5 ? 1.49,1,2,.5
INGREDIENT 6 ? .75,1,12,1
INGREDIENT 7 ? .40,1,4,.6666667
INGREDIENT 8 ? .49,1,1,3
NUMBER OF SERVINGS? 8

TOTAL COST FOR 1 RECIPE = $ 2.41
COST PER SERVING = $ .3

CHANGE NUMBER OF SERVINGS (1=YES,0=NO)? 1
NUMBER OF SERVINGS? 12

TOTAL COST FOR 1 RECIPE = $ 2.41
COST PER SERVING = $ .2

CHANGE NUMBER OF SERVINGS (1=YES,0=NO)? 0

END PROGRAM
```

PROGRAM LISTING

```
   1   REM - OPTION 55-70
  10   PRINT "RECIPE COST"
   .
   .
  50   FOR I=1  TO N
  55   REM - ENTER C,U,F,R
  56   REM - WHERE C=COST FOR BULK UNIT
  57   REM -       U=NUMBER UNITS IN BULK UNIT
  58   REM -       F=RECIPE UNITS PER BULK UNIT
  59   REM -       R=NUMBER RECIPE UNITS CALLED FOR
  60   PRINT "INGREDIENT";I;
  70   INPUT C,U,F,R
 149   REM - SUM COST OF EACH INGREDIENT PER AMOUNT USED
   .
   .
 260   END
```

Survey Check (Map Check)

Courtesy: Robert Irving
Northridge,
California

This program calculates the error of closure and area of a plot for which a traverse of the perimeter is available. The program will also calculate how far North and East the end of an open traverse is from its origin (the Northing and Easting). The local coordinates of the origin can be entered for an open traverse. Negative values of Northing and Easting are South and West, respectively, of the 0,0 origin of the survey.

The individual legs of the traverse may be either straight lines or arcs of circles. To compute the traverse, you must have the bearing and length of each straight leg. You also need the radius, bearing of chord, and length of chord (or radius, arc measure, and bearing of a tangent) for each curved leg.

For a closed survey, pick any intersection of legs as a starting point, and number the lines and arcs, starting with one, in a *clockwise* direction around the perimeter. If any arc is 180 degrees or more, it must be broken into smaller arcs, each less than 180 degrees.

By convention, surveyors measure bearings East and West of North and South, as shown in the following figure. This convention was established in the days before computers, so that trigonometric functions could be easily looked up in tables not exceeding 90 degrees. For each leg, you must enter the quadrant number and the degrees, minutes and seconds East or West of the North-South axis. The program will indicate the direction of the leg (e.g., SW), and will convert the quadrant, degrees, etc. to an azimuth angle. Azimuth is measured clockwise from North to 360 degrees.

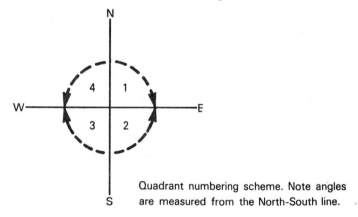

Quadrant numbering scheme. Note angles are measured from the North-South line.

A curved leg, or arc, is defined by two auxiliary legs, each of which is a radius of the arc. The bearing of the first auxiliary leg is the direction of the radius from the first encountered end of the arc to the center of the arc. You can compute this bearing from the bearing of the arc's tangent at that point, since the radius is perpendicular to the tangent. The survey may show the bearing of the tangent. If not, you can compute it by adding one half the angular extent of the arc to the bearing of the arc's chord, as shown in the next figure.

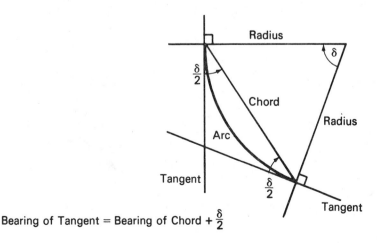

Bearing of Tangent = Bearing of Chord + $\frac{\delta}{2}$

177

The bearing of the second radius is from the center of the arc to the other end, and the distance is entered as a *negative* number to signal to the computer that this and the prior leg are not perimeter legs, but auxiliary legs of an arc.

The program asks you for the bearing and distance of each leg by number. Legs are entered in sets of ten (or less). Following the last entry in a set, you can correct any leg in the set. You must enter both auxiliary legs of an arc in the same set. You can enter a bearing of zero to end one set, and then enter more legs on the next set.

When you have corrected a set, a traverse table is printed for the set. This includes each leg number, direction, azimuth angle and distance, and incremental and cumulative Northing and Easting. The cumulative Northing and Easting after the last leg on a closed survey gives the error of closure. Arc angle, radius, sector area, chord length, and tangent length are printed between the two auxiliary legs of each curved leg.

Following the printout of the last leg of a closed survey, the area of the plot will be printed, both in square feet and in acres. The area computed is very accurate provided two conditions are met:

1) the error of closure is small (0.01 feet is usual for a house lot), and

2) the area is sufficiently small that curvature of the earth does not become significant. Surveys covering several tens of miles have to account for this latter factor.

Example:

The figure below illustrates the boundaries of a lot with one curved side. The leg numbers are circled. Bearings and distances are shown for each leg. Find the error of closure and lot area.

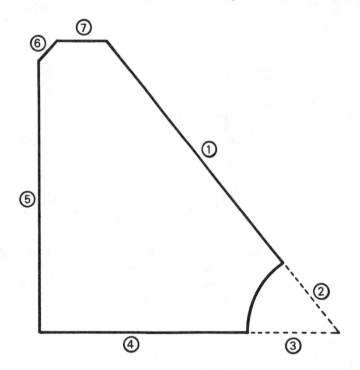

① S39°0"E
149.83
② S39°0"E
50.00
③ N85°23'53"W
50.00
④ N85°23'53"W
114.32
⑤ N1°5'0"E
132.78
⑥ N46°0'0"E
14.00
⑦ S89°0'0"E
25.46

```
:RUN
MAP CHECK - SURVEY CLOSURE & AREA
OPEN (1) OR CLOSED (0) SURVEY? 0
NEXT SET OF LEGS:
LEG NO.  1 :QUADRANT,DEGREES,MINUTES,SECONDS? 2,39,0,0
DISTANCE (NEGATIVE IF OUTWARD RADIUS)? 149.83
LEG NO.  2 :QUADRANT,DEGREES,MINUTES,SECONDS? 2,39,0,0
DISTANCE (NEGATIVE IF OUTWARD RADIUS)? 50
LEG NO.  3 :QUADRANT,DEGREES,MINUTES,SECONDS? 4,85,23,53
DISTANCE (NEGATIVE IF OUTWARD RADIUS)? -50
LEG NO.  4 :QUADRANT,DEGREES,MINUTES,SECONDS? 4,85,23,53
DISTANCE (NEGATIVE IF OUTWARD RADIUS)? 114.32
LEG NO.  5 :QUADRANT,DEGREES,MINUTES,SECONDS? 1,1,5,0
DISTANCE (NEGATIVE IF OUTWARD RADIUS)? 132.78
LEG NO.  6 :QUADRANT,DEGREES,MINUTES,SECONDS? 1,46,0,0
DISTANCE (NEGATIVE IF OUTWARD RADIUS)? 14
LEG NO.  7 :QUADRANT,DEGREES,MINUTES,SECONDS? 2,89,0,0
DISTANCE (NEGATIVE IF OUTWARD RADIUS)? 25.46
LEG NO.  8 :QUADRANT,DEGREES,MINUTES,SECONDS? 0,0,0,0
CORRECT WHICH LEG IN THIS SET (0=NO MORE CHANGES)? 0

LEG/DIR.   AZIMUTH/DIST.             DEL N/DEL E    NORTHING/EASTING
                                                        0 / 0

 1 /SE  141  0   0 / 149.83          -116.44 / 94.291 -116.44 / 94.291

 2 /SE  141  0   0 / 50              -38.857 / 31.466 -155.297 / 125.757

    ARC:  46  23   53 R= 50 A= 2024.497 C= 39.393 T= 21.429

 3 /NW  274  36   7 / 50             4.012 /-49.839 -151.285 / 75.918

 4 /NW  274  36   7 / 114.32         9.172 /-113.951 -142.113 /-38.033

 5 /NE  1   4  60 / 132.78           132.756 / 2.51 -9.357 /-35.523

 6 /NE  46  0   0 / 14               9.725 / 10.071   .368 /-25.452

 7 /SE  91  0   0 / 25.46            -.444 / 25.456 -7.60E-02 / 4.0E-03

ANY MORE LEGS (1=YES, 0=NO)? 0
PLOT AREA IS   13347.683 SQ. FT.

PLOT AREA IS   .30642064 ACRES

STOP
```

```
  3    REM - MAP CHECK & AREA OF PLOT
  4    REM - FOR CLOSED SURVEY FOLLOW TRAVERSE CLOCKWISE
  5    REM - KEEP PLOT TO RIGHT OF EACH PERIMETER LEG
  6    REM - COMPUTE AUXILIARY LEGS AS RADII AT EACH
  7    REM - END OF ARC.  ARC < 180 DEGREES
  8    REM
  9    REM - VALUE OF PI
 10    P1=3.141592654
 14    REM - K0 = NO. OF LEGS PER SET
 15    K0=10
 20    DIM B(10),L(10)
 29    REM - C0$ CONTAINS 'CLEAR SCREEN' CHARACTER
 30    C0$=HEX(03)
 39    REM - FNR(X) ROUNDS X TO 3 DECIMAL PLACES
 40    DEFFNR(X)=INT(X*1000+.5)/1000
 49    REM - R IS CONVERSION FACTOR FOR DEGREES TO RADIANS
 50    R=1.745329251E-2
 60    PRINT C0$;"MAP CHECK - SURVEY CLOSURE & AREA"
 70    PRINT "OPEN (1) OR CLOSED (0) SURVEY";
 80    INPUT F
 90    IF F=0  THEN  120
100    PRINT "ORIGIN: NORTHING ,EASTING";
110    INPUT N,E
120    PRINT C0$;"NEXT SET OF LEGS:"
125    G=H
130    FOR  K=1  TO K0
139    REM - INPUT BEARING AND DISTANCE FOR NEXT LEG
140    GOSUB 2000
149    REM - IF BEARING IS 0, END INPUT FOR THIS SET
150    IF Q=0  THEN  170
155    G=G+1
160    GOTO  240
169    REM - ZERO UNUSED LEGS IN THIS SET
170    IF K=K0  THEN  230
180    FOR J=K+1  TO K0
190    B(J)=0
200    L(J)=0
210    NEXT J
230    K=K0
240    NEXT K
260    PRINT "CORRECT WHICH LEG IN THIS SET (0=NO MORE CHANGES)";
270    INPUT K
279    REM - NO CHANGES IF 0 INPUT
280    IF K=0  THEN  310
285    K=K-H
290    GOSUB 2000
300    GOTO  260
309    REM - COMPUTE VALUES AND PRINT TRAVERSE TABLE
310    PRINT
315    PRINT "LEG/DIR.  AZIMUTH/DIST.";
320    PRINT "          DEL N/DEL E    NORTHING/EASTING"
330    PRINT ,,,FNR(N);"/";FNR(E)
340    PRINT
350    FOR K=1  TO K0
360    L1=L(K)
```

```
369   REM - CHECK FOR ARC
370   IF L1<0    THEN 1100
380   IF L1=0    THEN   900
388   REM - COMPUTE NORTHING/EASTING INCREMENT (CONVERT
389   REM - BEARINGS FROM DEGREES TO RADIANS)
390   L=L(K)*COS(B(K)*R)
400   D=L(K)*SIN(B(K)*R)
410   N=N+L
420   E=E+D
429   REM - INCREMENT AREA
430   A=A-E*L+N*D
440   PRINT H+K;"/";
449   REM - FROM BEARING, DETERMINE DIRECTION
450   IF B(K)=0    THEN   470
460   GOTO   490
470   PRINT "N";
480   GOTO   830
490   IF B(K)<90    THEN   510
500   GOTO   530
510   PRINT "NE";
520   GOTO   830
530   IF B(K)=90    THEN   550
540   GOTO   570
550   PRINT "E ";
560   GOTO   830
570   IF B(K)<180    THEN   590
580   GOTO   610
590   PRINT "SE";
600   GOTO   830
610   IF B(K)=180    THEN   630
620   GOTO   650
630   PRINT "S ";
640   GOTO   830
650   IF B(K)<270    THEN   670
660   GOTO   690
670   PRINT "SW";
680   GOTO   830
690   IF B(K)=270    THEN   710
700   GOTO   730
710   PRINT "W ";
720   GOTO   830
730   IF B(K)<360    THEN   750
740   GOTO   770
750   PRINT "NW";
760   GOTO   830
770   IF B(K)=360    THEN   790
780   GOTO   810
790   PRINT "N ";
800   GOTO   830
810   B(K)=B(K)-360
820   GOTO   450
829   REM - BREAK BEARING INTO DEGREES, MINUTES, SECONDS
830   D1=INT(B(K))
840   M1=(B(K)-D1)*60
850   M=INT(M1)
860   S=INT((M1-M)*60+.5)
870   PRINT " ";D1;M;S;"/";FNR(L(K)),FNR(L);
```

```
880    PRINT "/";FNR(D);FNR(N);"/";FNR(E)
885    PRINT
890    L(K)=L1
900    NEXT K
910    H=G
920    PRINT "ANY MORE LEGS (1=YES, 0=NO)";
930    INPUT U
940    IF U<>0   THEN  120
949    REM - NO AREA FOR OPEN SURVEY
950    IF F<>0   THEN 1000
960    A=ABS(A/2)
970    PRINT "PLOT AREA IS ";FNR(A);"SQ. FT."
980    PRINT
990    PRINT "PLOT AREA IS ";INT(A/43560*1E8+.5)/1E8;"ACRES"
1000   STOP
1099   REM - CALCULATE CURVED LEG AND PRINT ON TRAVERSE TABLE
1100   C=ABS(B(K)-B(K-1))
1110   C=ABS(180-C)
1120   D=-L1
1130   L(K)=D
1140   A1=C/180*P1*D*D
1150   C1=2*D*SIN(C/2*R)
1160   T=D*TAN(C/2*R)
1170   B9=B(K)-B(K-1)
1180   IF B9<-180   THEN 1230
1190   IF B9>180   THEN 1210
1200   IF B9>0   THEN  1230
1210   A=A+A1
1220   GOTO 1240
1230   A=A-A1
1240   D1=INT(C)
1250   M1=(C-D1)*60
1260   M=INT(M1)
1270   S=INT((M1-M)*60+.5)
1280   PRINT "   ARC: ";D1;M;S;"R=";FNR(D);"A=";FNR(A1);"C=";
1290   PRINT FNR(C1);"T=";FNR(T)
1300   PRINT
1320   GOTO  390
1999   REM - INPUT DATA FOR ONE LEG
2000   B(K)=0
2010   L(K)=0
2020   PRINT "LEG NO. ";H+K;":QUADRANT,DEGREES,MINUTES,SECONDS";
2030   INPUT Q,D,M,S
2040   IF Q=0   THEN 2270
2050   IF Q>4   THEN 2020
2060   IF Q<0   THEN 2020
2070   IF D<0   THEN 2020
2080   IF M<0   THEN 2020
2090   IF S<0   THEN 2020
2100   B(K)=D+(M+S/60)/60
2110   IF B(K)>90   THEN  2020
2120   IF Q=1   THEN 2220
2130   IF Q=2   THEN 2150
2140   GOTO 2170
2150   B(K)=180-B(K)
2160   GOTO 2220
2170   IF Q=3   THEN 2190
```

```
2180   GOTO 2210
2190   B(K)=180+B(K)
2200   GOTO 2220
2210   IF Q<>4   THEN 2220
2215   B(K)=360-B(K)
2220   PRINT "DISTANCE (NEGATIVE IF OUTWARD RADIUS)";
2230   INPUT L(K)
2240   IF L(K)>0   THEN 2270
2250   IF ABS(L(K))<>ABS(L(K-1))   THEN 2220
2270   RETURN
9999   END
```

Day of the Week

This program calculates the day of the week that a given date falls on. It will figure, for example, that December 25, 1980 will be a Thursday.

You must enter the date in numeric form and in the order of month, day, year. September 12, 1975 will be entered as `9,12,1975`, making certain that commas, not slashes or dashes, separate the figures.

Examples:

Cindy's birthdate is March 4, 1953. On what day was she born?

Uncle Lon has an appointment on September 30, 1977. What day is that on?

```
:RUN
DAY OF THE WEEK

(ENTER 0,0,0 TO END PROGRAM)
MONTH, DAY, YEAR? 3,4,1953
WEDNESDAY

MONTH, DAY, YEAR? 9,30,1977
FRIDAY

MONTH, DAY, YEAR? 0,0,0

END PROGRAM


PROGRAM LISTING

  10   PRINT "DAY OF THE WEEK"
  20   PRINT
  29   REM - REQUEST USER INPUT
  30   PRINT "(ENTER 0,0,0 TO END PROGRAM)"
  40   PRINT  "MONTH, DAY, YEAR";
  50   INPUT M,D,Y
  59   REM - TEST FOR END OF PROGRAM
  60   IF M<>0  THEN  100
  70   IF D<>0  THEN  100
  80   IF Y<>0  THEN  100
  90   GOTO  360
  99   REM - NEED TO ADJUST INPUT FOR CALCULATIONS?
 100   IF M>2  THEN  130
 109   REM - ADJUST INPUT
 110   M=M+12
 120   Y=Y-1
 129   REM - CALCULATE DAY NUMBER
 130   N=D+2*M+INT(.6*(M+1))+Y+INT(Y/4)-INT(Y/100)+INT(Y/400)+2
 140   N=INT((N/7-INT(N/7))*7+.5)
 149   REM - FIND CORRECT DAY NUMBER, TRANSLATE TO DAY, PRINT
 150   IF N>0  THEN  180
 160   PRINT "SATURDAY"
 170   GOTO  340
```

```
180    IF N>1   THEN   210
190    PRINT  "SUNDAY"
200    GOTO   340
210    IF N>2   THEN   240
220    PRINT  "MONDAY"
230    GOTO   340
240    IF N>3   THEN   270
250    PRINT  "TUESDAY"
260    GOTO   340
270    IF N>4   THEN   300
280    PRINT  "WEDNESDAY"
290    GOTO   340
300    IF N>5   THEN   330
310    PRINT  "THURSDAY"
320    GOTO   340
330    PRINT  "FRIDAY"
340    PRINT
349    REM - RESTART PROGRAM
350    GOTO    40
360    END
```

Days between Two Dates

This program calculates the number of days between two given dates. Leap years are taken into account. The program assumes there is one day between today and tomorrow. For instance, there are two days between March 1 and March 3 of the same year.

There are a few precautions to assure the proper use of this program. First, you must be certain to enter the earlier date first. Second, dates must be entered in number form (3, not MARCH) and in the correct order (month, day, year, i.e., 3,17,1976). Commas, not slashes or dashes, must separate the figures. Third, the year must not be abbreviated (1976 , not 76), even if both dates are in the same century. Finally, the month entered must not be greater than 12 and the days no greater than the number of days in the particular month. If such is the case, the message UNREAL DATE is printed to alert you to the fact that an unreal date (such as 14,32,1975) has been entered. An incorrect answer is likely to result.

Example:

John's birthdate is August 8, 1951. How many days old will he be on his 30th birthday?

```
:RUN
DAYS BETWEEN TWO DATES

FIRST DATE? 8,8,1951
SECOND DATE? 8,8,1981
DIFFERENCE = 10958 DAYS

MORE DATA (1=YES, 0=NO)? 0

END PROGRAM


PROGRAM LISTING

    10    PRINT "DAYS BETWEEN TWO DATES"
    20    PRINT
    29    REM - STATEMENTS 30 TO 60 REQUEST USER INPUT
    30    PRINT "FIRST DATE";
    40    INPUT M1,D1,Y1
    50    PRINT "SECOND DATE";
    60    INPUT M2,D2,Y2
    69    REM - SET VARIABLES TO BE USED IN SUBROUTINE
    70    M=M1
    80    D=D1
    90    Y=Y1
   100    GOSUB  230
   109    REM - SAVE COMPUTED NUMBER OF DAYS IN N
   110    N=A
   119    REM - SET VARIABLES TO BE USED IN SUBROUTINE
   120    M=M2
   130    D=D2
   140    Y=Y2
```

```
150    GOSUB   230
159    REM - CALCULATE DIFFERENCE AND PRINT
160    N=A-N
170    PRINT "DIFFERENCE =";N;"DAYS"
180    PRINT
189    REM - RESTART OR END PROGRAM?
190    PRINT "MORE DATA (1=YES, 0=NO)";
200    INPUT X
210    IF X=1  THEN    20
219    REM - END PROGRAM
220    GOTO  460
227    REM - SUBROUTINE TO COMPUTE NUMBER OF DAYS SINCE 0,0,0 TO M,D,Y
228    REM - START WITH TEST FOR UNREAL DATE
229    REM - GO TO CORRECT TEST DEPENDING ON NUMBER OF DAYS IN MONTH
230    ON M GOTO  260 , 280 , 260 , 340 , 260 , 340 , 260 , 260 , 340 ,
       260 , 340 , 260
239    REM - IF THIS MESSAGE IS PRINTED THE ANSWER IS PROBABLY INCORRECT
240    PRINT "UNREAL DATE"
249    REM - STOP CALCULATIONS, RETURN TO MAIN PROGRAM
250    RETURN
259    REM - MONTH HAS 31 DAYS
260    IF D>31  THEN   240
270    GOTO  350
279    REM - MONTH IS FEBRUARY; A LEAP YEAR?
280    IF Y/4<>INT(Y/4)  THEN   310
290    IF Y/400=INT(Y/400)  THEN   320
300    IF Y/100<>INT(Y/100)  THEN   320
309    REM - NOT A LEAP YEAR; MONTH HAS 28 DAYS
310    IF D>28  THEN   240
319    REM - A LEAP YEAR; MONTH HAS 29 DAYS
320    IF D>29  THEN   240
330    GOTO  350
339    REM - MONTH HAS 30 DAYS
340    IF D>30  THEN   240
349    REM - TABLE OF NUMBER OF DAYS FROM 1ST OF YEAR TO 1ST OF EACH MON
    TH
350    DATA 0,31,59,90,120,151,181,212,243,273,304,334
360    RESTORE
365    FOR H=1  TO M
369    REM - GET NUMBER OF DAYS FROM JAN 1 TO 1ST OF MONTH FROM DATA TAB
    LE
370    READ A
375    NEXT H
379    REM - COMPUTE NUMBER OF DAYS FROM 0,0,0 TO M,D,Y
380    A=A+Y*365+INT(Y/4)+D+1-INT(Y/100)+INT(Y/400)
389    REM - POSSIBLY A LEAP YEAR?
390    IF INT(Y/4)<>Y/4  THEN   450
409    REM - CONTINUE TEST FOR LEAP YEAR
410    IF Y/400=INT(Y/400)  THEN   430
420    IF Y/100=INT(Y/100)  THEN   450
428    REM - YEAR IS A LEAP YEAR;
429    REM - IF MONTH IS JAN OR FEB ADJUST CALCULATED NUMBER OF DAYS
430    IF M>2  THEN   450
440    A=A-1
449    REM - END OF SUBROUTINE, RETURN TO MAIN PROGRAM
450    RETURN
460    END
```

OPTION

To shorten this program you may wish to omit the test for unreal dates. It should be noted that if a month of more than 12 is entered when this test is omitted, an input error will result. The program lines which may be deleted are listed following the example below.

Example:

How many days are there between July 4 and Christmas?

```
:RUN
DAYS BETWEEN TWO DATES

FIRST DATE? 7,4,1977
SECOND DATE? 12,25,1977
DIFFERENCE = 174 DAYS

MORE DATA (1=YES, 0=NO)? 0

END PROGRAM
```

```
PROGRAM LISTING

  10    PRINT "DAYS BETWEEN TWO DATES"
   .
   .
   .
  90    Y=Y1
 100    GOSUB  350
 109    REM - SAVE COMPUTED NUMBER OF DAYS IN N
   .
   .
   .
 140    Y=Y2
 150    GOSUB  350
 159    REM - CALCULATE DIFFERENCE AND PRINT
   .
   .
   .
 227    REM - SUBROUTINE TO COMPUTE NUMBER OF DAYS SINCE 0,0,0 TO M,D,Y
(Delete lines 228 - 340)
 349    REM - TABLE OF NUMBER OF DAYS FROM 1ST OF YEAR TO 1ST OF EACH MON
        TH
   .
   .
   .
 460    END
```

Anglo to Metric

This program converts a measure given in anglo units to metric units. The conversions available in this program are as follows:

1. Inches to centimeters
2. Feet to centimeters
3. Feet to meters
4. Yards to meters
5. Miles to kilometers
6. Teaspoons to cubic centimeters
7. Tablespoons to cubic centimeters
8. Cups to liters
9. Pints to liters
10. Quarts to liters
11. Gallons to liters
12. Bushels to liters
13. Pecks to liters
14. Ounces to grams
15. Pounds to kilograms
16. Tons to kilograms
17. Degrees Fahrenheit to degrees Celsius

You must provide the value of the anglo measurement and the number of the conversion (1 - 17 as listed above) which you wish to perform.

Example:

Perform the following conversions:

8.5	miles to kilometers
75°	Fahrenheit to degrees Celsius
10	gallons to liters

```
:RUN
ANGLO TO METRIC

(TO END PROGRAM ENTER 0)
WHICH CONVERSION DO YOU NEED? 5
VALUE TO BE CONVERTED? 8.5
 8.5 MILES = 13.6765 KILOMETERS

WHICH CONVERSION DO YOU NEED? 17
VALUE TO BE CONVERTED? 75
 75 DEGREES FAHRENHEIT = 23.88888888889 CELSIUS

WHICH CONVERSION DO YOU NEED? 11
VALUE TO BE CONVERTED? 10
 10 GALLONS = 37.85 LITERS

WHICH CONVERSION DO YOU NEED? 0

END PROGRAM
```

```
10    PRINT "ANGLO TO METRIC"
20    PRINT
29    REM - ESTABLISH VARIABLES FOR 17 CONVERSION FACTORS
30    DIM C(17)
39    REM - LOOP TO ASSIGN CONVERSION FACTORS INTO C( )
40    FOR N=1  TO 17
50    READ C(N)
60    NEXT N
69    REM - DATA TABLE OF SEVENTEEN CONVERSION FACTORS
70    DATA 2.540,30.480,.3048,.9144,1.609,4.929,14.788,.2366,.4732
80    DATA .9463,3.785,35.24,8.809,28.3495,.4536,907.2,.6214
89    REM - GET NUMBER OF CONVERSION FROM PROGRAM DESCRIPTION
90    PRINT "(TO END PROGRAM ENTER 0)"
100   PRINT "WHICH CONVERSION DO YOU NEED";
110   INPUT N
119   REM - END PROGRAM?
120   IF N=0  THEN  540
129   REM - CONVERSION AVAILABLE?
130   IF N>17  THEN  100
140   PRINT "VALUE TO BE CONVERTED";
150   INPUT I
159   REM - PERFORM CONVERSION USING PROPER CONVERSION FACTOR
160   R=I*C(N)
169   REM - DIRECT PROGRAM TO PROPER CONVERSION UNITS, PRINT RESULTS
170   ON N GOTO  180 , 200 , 220 , 240 , 260 , 280 , 300 , 320 , 340 ,
      360 , 380 , 400 , 420 , 440 ,  460 , 480 , 500
180   PRINT I;"INCHES =";R;"CENTIMETERS"
190   GOTO  520
200   PRINT I;"FEET =";R;"CENTIMETERS"
210   GOTO  520
220   PRINT I;"FEET =";R;"METERS"
230   GOTO  520
240   PRINT I;"YARDS =";R;"METERS"
250   GOTO  520
260   PRINT I;"MILES =";R;"KILOMETERS"
270   GOTO  520
280   PRINT I;"TSP. =";R;"CUBIC CENTIMETERS"
290   GOTO  520
300   PRINT I;"TBSP. =";R;"CUBIC CENTIMETERS"
310   GOTO  520
320   PRINT I;"CUPS =";R;"LITERS"
330   GOTO  520
340   PRINT I;"PINTS =";R;"LITERS"
350   GOTO  520
360   PRINT I;"QUARTS =";R;"LITERS"
370   GOTO  520
380   PRINT I;"GALLONS =";R;"LITERS"
390   GOTO  520
400   PRINT I;"BUSHELS =";R;"LITERS"
410   GOTO  520
420   PRINT I;"PECKS =";R;"LITERS"
430   GOTO  520
440   PRINT I;"OUNCES =";R;"GRAMS"
450   GOTO  520
460   PRINT I;"POUNDS =";R;"KILOGRAMS"
```

```
470    GOTO  520
480    PRINT I;"TONS =";R;"KILOGRAMS"
490    GOTO  520
499    REM - CONVERT FROM DEGREES FARENHEIT TO CELSIUS
500    R=(I-32)*5/9
510    PRINT I;"DEGREES FAHRENHEIT =";R;"CELSIUS"
520    PRINT
529    REM - RESTART PROGRAM
530    GOTO  100
540    END
```

Alphabetize

This program alphabetizes a list of words or phrases.

Numbers may be part of an alphanumeric phrase. However, they will not be put into numeric order unless they contain the same number of digits. Numbers with fewer digits must be justified to the right by prefixing zeros. Thus, if the numbers you are sorting range into the hundreds, the number 13 would be entered as 013.

To save memory space, the array at statement 70 should be limited to the maximum number of terms you wish alphabetized. The dimension statement should be altered in the following manner:

$$70 \ \text{DIM A\$}(N)$$

where N = the number of items to be alphabetized.

Example:

Alphabetize the following names:

> Robert Wilson
> Susan W. James
> Kent Smith
> Michael Mitchell
> Ann T. McGowan
> Alexander Lee II
> Mary Mitchell
> David Bowers
> Steven Evans
> Carol Jameson
> Linda North

```
:70 DIM A$(11)
:RUN
ALPHABETIZE

(TO END PROGRAM ENTER 0)
NUMBER OF ITEMS? 11
ITEM 1 ? WILSON ROBERT
ITEM 2 ? JAMES SUSAN W.
ITEM 3 ? SMITH KENT
ITEM 4 ? MITCHELL MICHAEL
ITEM 5 ? MCGOWAN ANN T.
ITEM 6 ? LEE ALEXANDER II
ITEM 7 ? MITCHELL MARY
ITEM 8 ? BOWERS DAVID
ITEM 9 ? EVANS STEVEN
ITEM 10 ? JAMESON CAROL
ITEM 11 ? NORTH LINDA
BOWERS DAVID
EVANS STEVEN
JAMES SUSAN W.
JAMESON CAROL
LEE ALEXANDER II
MCGOWAN ANN T.
```

```
MITCHELL MARY
MITCHELL MICHAEL
NORTH LINDA
SMITH KENT
WILSON ROBERT

NUMBER OF ITEMS? 0

END PROGRAM


PROGRAM LISTING

  10    PRINT "ALPHABETIZE"
  20    PRINT
  30    PRINT "(TO END PROGRAM ENTER 0)"
  40    PRINT "NUMBER OF ITEMS";
  50    INPUT N
  60    IF N=0  THEN  330
  69    REM -LIMIT ARRAY TO MAXIMUM NUMBER OF ITEMS TO BE ENTERED IN ONE RUN
  70    DIM A$(25)
  80    FOR I=1  TO N
  90    PRINT "ITEM";I;
 100    INPUT A$(I)
 110    NEXT I
 120    M=N
 128    REM - THE SORT TECHNIQUE USED COMPARES DATA ITEMS IN DIMINISHING INC
        REMENTS.
 129    REM - THE FIRST PASS COMPARES ITEMS N/2 ELEMENTS APART, THE SECOND
        (N/2)/2 ELEMENTS APART, AND SO ON UNTIL THE INCREMENT IS EXHAUSTED.
 130    M=INT(M/2)
 140    IF M=0  THEN  280
 150    K=N-M
 160    J=1
 170    I=J
 180    L=I+M
 190    IF A$(I)<=A$(L)  THEN  250
 200    T$=A$(I)
 210    A$(I)=A$(L)
 220    A$(L)=T$
 230    I=I-M
 240    IF I>=1  THEN  180
 250    J=J+1
 260    IF J>K  THEN  130
 270    GOTO  170
 280    FOR I=1  TO N
 290    PRINT A$(I)
 300    NEXT I
 310    PRINT
 320    GOTO    40
 330    END
```

OPTION

   You may wish your list alphabetized in reverse, or from highest to lowest. The program changes necessary
are listed following the example below.

Example:

The scores on a math test range from 82 to 117. Put the students in order according to their scores, from highest to lowest.

```
 89  Bowers
102  Evans
111  James
100  Jameson
 99  Lee
117  McGowan
102  Mitchell
 82  Mitchell
 97  North
 91  Smith
108  Wilson
```

```
:70 DIM A$(11)
:RUN
ALPHABETIZE

(TO END PROGRAM ENTER 0)
NUMBER OF ITEMS? 11
ITEM 1 ? 089 BOWERS
ITEM 2 ? 102 EVANS
ITEM 3 ? 111 JAMES
ITEM 4 ? 100 JAMESON
ITEM 5 ? 099 LEE
ITEM 6 ? 117 MCGOWAN
ITEM 7 ? 102 MITCHELL
ITEM 8 ? 082 MITCHELL
ITEM 9 ? 097 NORTH
ITEM 10 ? 091 SMITH
ITEM 11 ? 108 WILSON
117 MCGOWAN
111 JAMES
108 WILSON
102 MITCHELL
102 EVANS
100 JAMESON
099 LEE
097 NORTH
091 SMITH
089 BOWERS
082 MITCHELL

NUMBER OF ITEMS? 0

END PROGRAM


PROGRAM LISTING
    1    REM - OPTION 190
   10    PRINT "ALPHABETIZE"
   .
   .
  180    L=I+M
  190    IF A$(I)>=A$(L)  THEN  250
  200    T$=A$(I)
   .
   .
  330    END
```

194

References

Mendenhall, William, et al., *Statistics: A Tool for the Social Sciences.* North Scituate,
Massachusetts: Duxbury Press, 1974.

Paige, Lowell J. and J. Dean Swift, *Elements of Linear Algebra.*
Boston: Ginn and Company, 1961.

Sakarovitch, M., *Notes on Linear Programming.*
New York: Van Nostrand Reinhold Company, 1971.

Spiegel, Murray R., *Theory and Problems of Statistics.*
New York: Schaum's Outline Series, Schaum Publishing Company, 1961.

Thomas, George B., Jr., *Calculus and Analytic Geometry,*
part one, 4th ed. Reading Massachusetts: Addison-Wesley Publishing
Company, 1968.

U.S. Department of Commerce, *Handbook of Mathematical Functions.*
National Bureau of Standards, Applied Mathematics Series 55, 1964.

Conversions of OSBORNE/McGraw-Hill's **Some Common BASIC Programs** are being made so the 76 programs are ready to run on many popular systems. A conversion is available from OSBORNE on cassette for the Commodore PET, and conversions will soon be released on cassette and disk for a variety of systems. Independent consultants and businesses are also marketing their own conversions. For further information about these magnetic surfaces, fill out the form below and mail it to OSBORNE/McGraw-Hill (a photocopy of the form will do).

Cut out and mail this request form to:

Some Common BASIC Programs Conversions
OSBORNE/McGraw-Hill
630 Bancroft Way
Berkeley, California   94710

Please send further information regarding conversions of **Some Common BASIC Programs** for the following:

Name:_____

Street:_____

City:_____

State:_____ Zip:_____

☐ Commodore PET

☐ TRS-80 Level II

☐ Other microcomputer

System:_____